Houghton Mifflin
Math

 HOUGHTON MIFFLIN   BOSTON

Program Authors & Consultants

Authors

Dr. Carole Greenes

Professor of Mathematics Education

Boston University
Boston, MA

Dr. Matt Larson

Curriculum Specialist for Mathematics

Lincoln Public Schools
Lincoln, NE

Dr. Miriam A. Leiva

Distinguished Professor of Mathematics Emerita

University of
North Carolina
Charlotte, NC

Dr. Jean M. Shaw

Professor Emerita of Curriculum and Instruction

University of Mississippi
Oxford, MS

Dr. Lee Stiff

Professor of Mathematics Education

North Carolina State University
Raleigh, NC

Dr. Bruce R. Vogeli

Clifford Brewster Upton Professor of Mathematics

Teachers College, Columbia University
New York, NY

Dr. Karol Yeatts

Associate Professor

Barry University
Miami, FL

Consultants

Strategic Consultant
Dr. Liping Ma

Senior Scholar

Carnegie Foundation for the Advancement of Technology
Palo Alto, CA

Language and Vocabulary Consultant
Dr. David Chard

Professor of Reading

University of Oregon
Eugene, OR

Reviewers

Grade K

Hilda Kendrick
W E Wilson
Elementary School
Jefferson, IN

Debby Nagel
Assumption
Elementary School
Cincinnati, OH

Jen Payet
Lake Ave. Elementary School
Saratoga Springs, NY

Karen Sue Hinton
Washington Elementary School
Ponca City, OK

Grade 1

Karen Wood
Clay Elementary School
Clay, AL

Paula Rowland
Bixby North Elementary School
Bixby, OK

Stephanie McDaniel
B. Everett Jordan
Elementary School
Graham, NC

Juan Melgar
Lowrie Elementary School
Elgin, IL

Sharon O'Brien
Echo Mountain School
Phoenix, AZ

Grade 2

Sally Bales
Akron Elementary School
Akron, IN

Rose Marie Bruno
Mawbey Street Elementary
School
Woodbridge, NJ

Kiesha Doster
Berry Elementary School
Detroit, MI

Marci Galazkiewicz
North Elementary School
Waukegan, IL

Ana Gaspar
Lowrie Elementary School
Elgin, IL

Elana Heinoren
Beechfield Elementary School
Baltimore, MD

Kim Terry
Woodland Elementary School
West
Gages Lake, IL

Megan Burton
Valley Elementary School
Pelham, AL

Kristy Ford
Eisenhower Elementary School
Norman, OK

Grade 3

Jenny Chang
North Elementary School
Waukegan, IL

Patricia Heintz
Harry T. Stewart
Elementary School
Corona, NY

Shannon Hopper
White Lick Elementary School
Brownsburg, IN

Allison White
Kingsley Elementary School
Naperville, IL

Amy Simpson
Broadmoore Elementary School
Moore, OK

Reviewers

Grade 4

Barbara O'Hanlon
Maurice & Everett Haines
Elementary School
Medford, NJ

Connie Rapp
Oakland Elementary School
Bloomington, IL

Pam Rettig
Solheim Elementary School
Bismarck, ND

Tracy Smith
Blanche Kelso Bruce Academy
Detroit, MI

Brenda Hancock
Clay Elementary School
Clay, AL

Karen Scroggins
Rock Quarry Elementary School
Tuscaloosa, AL

Lynn Fox
Kendall-Whittier Elementary
School
Tulsa, OK

Grade 5

Jim Archer
Maplewood Elementary School
Indianapolis, IN

Maggie Dunning
Horizon Elementary School
Hanover Park, IL

Mike Intoccia
McNichols Plaza
Scranton, PA

Jennifer LaBelle
Washington Elementary School
Waukegan, IL

Anne McDonald
St. Luke The Evangelist School
Glenside, PA

Ellen O'Rourke
Bower Elementary School
Warrenville, IL

Gary Smith
Thomas H. Ford Elementary
School
Reading, PA

Linda Carlson
Van Buren Elementary School
Oklahoma City, OK

Grade 6

Robin Akers
Sonoran Sky Elementary School
Scottsdale, AZ

Ellen Greenman
Daniel Webster Middle School
Waukegan, IL

Angela McCray
Abbott Middle School
West Bloomfield, MI

Mary Popovich
Horizon Elementary School
Hanover Park, IL

Debbie Taylor
Sonoran Sky Elementary School
Scottsdale, AZ

Across Grades

Jacqueline Lampley
Hewitt Elementary School
Trussville, AL

Rose Smith
Five Points Elementary School
Orrville, AL

Winnie Tepper
Morgan County Schools
Decatur, AL

Algebra Indicates lessons that include algebra instruction.

WR Indicates WEEKLY WR READER® Connection

Addition and Subtraction Facts Through 10 . 119a

STARTING THE UNIT

Ways to Add

Count on
Use a number line
Use doubles
Use counters
Draw a picture

Algebra Indicates lessons that include algebra instruction.

UNIT 3 Geometry and Fractions

x

Algebra Indicates lessons that include algebra instruction.

WR Indicates **WEEKLY WR READER® Connection**

Algebra Indicates lessons that include algebra instruction.

WR Indicates **WEEKLY WR READER® Connection**

Time and Money

STARTING THE UNIT

13 Time and Calendar

Algebra Indicates lessons that include algebra instruction.

FINISHING THE UNIT

WR Indicates **WEEKLY WR READER® Connection**

Addition and Subtraction Facts Through 12

STARTING THE UNIT

15   Addition Facts Through 12

Algebra Indicates lessons that include algebra instruction.

(WR) Indicates **WEEKLY** WR **READER** Connection

Measurement

Algebra Indicates lessons that include algebra instruction.

FINISHING THE UNIT

WR Indicates **WEEKLY WR READER® Connection**

Two-Digit Addition and Subtraction 551a

STARTING THE UNIT

19 Addition Facts Through 20 555

20 Subtraction Facts Through 20 579

UNIT 8 Two-Digit Addition and Subtraction

xx

Algebra Indicates lessons that include algebra instruction.

(WR) Indicates **WEEKLY WR READER® Connection**

Houghton Mifflin Math

Welcome To Grade 1 Math

Your book will help you learn about numbers, shapes, graphs, and patterns.

You will start with things you already know—counting, sorting, and ordering. You will learn about adding, subtracting, and solving problems.

You will work with your teacher and classmates to understand math.

Taking Tests

You will show what you have learned about math on math tests.

When you take a test, you need to know how to think about the math and how to take a test.

As you work on the lessons, you will see this special sign near **Explain Your Thinking**.

 This sign points out questions that help you think about math.

Some hints for reading problems

★ **Always read the problem twice. First, to understand the question. Then, to find information.**

★ **Make a picture of the problem on paper or in your mind to help you think about the question.**

Some pages in your book have special signs that help you practice taking tests.

You will find **TEST PREP** where you will practice listening to test questions.

You can use a **Practice Test** to see what taking a test is like.

These pages will help you get ready for real tests.

Some hints for taking tests

★ Listen carefully while your teacher reads the question.

★ If you are not sure how to answer a question, go on to the next one.

★ Reread the problem to make sure you have answered the question.

★ Be careful to fill in the space for the answer you want.

Number Concepts, Operations, and Graphing

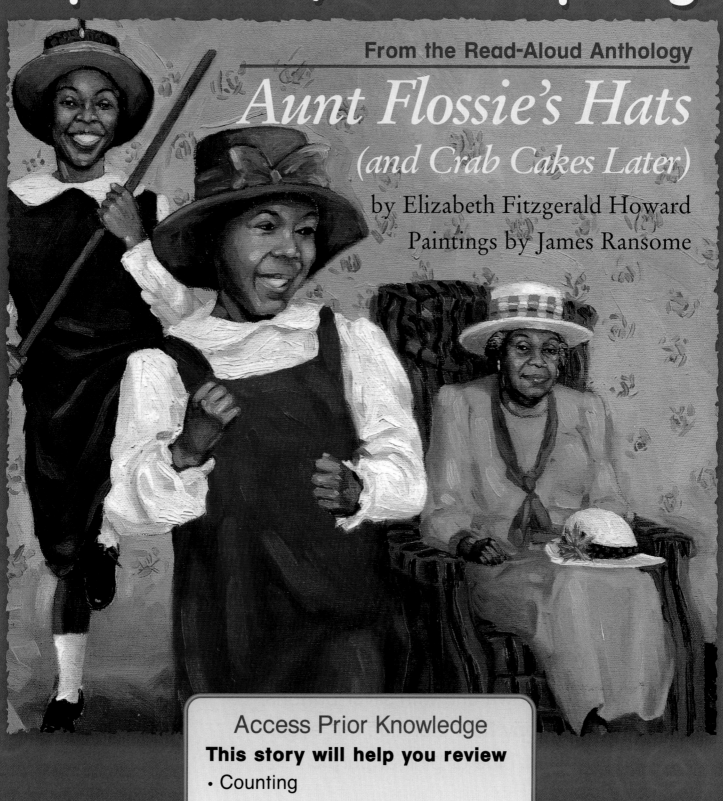

From the Read-Aloud Anthology

Aunt Flossie's Hats
(and Crab Cakes Later)

by Elizabeth Fitzgerald Howard

Paintings by James Ransome

Access Prior Knowledge
This story will help you review
- Counting
- Addition and subtraction concepts

Hats, hats, hats, hats!
A stiff black one with bright red ribbons.
A soft brown one with silver buttons.
Thin floppy hats that hide our eyes.
Green or blue or pink or purple.

1 b from *Aunt Flossie's Hats (and Crab Cakes Later)*

Some have fur and some have feathers.
Look! This hat is just one smooth soft rose,
but here's one with a trillion flowers!
Aunt Flossie has so many hats!

Name _____

Use the pictures on pages 1b and 1c.
Count.

1. How many hats are being worn?   _____ hats

2. How many hats are not being worn?   _____ hat

3. How many hats are there altogether?   _____ hats

4. If you were in the picture with a hat, how many hats would there be?

   Draw a picture of yourself wearing a hat.

   _____ hats

5. **Create Your Own** Aunt Flossie has many kinds of hats. What kind of hat would you like to have? Decorate your own hat using **5** or fewer things.

   How many things did you draw on your hat? _____

2

Dear Family,

My class is starting Unit 1. I will be learning about numbers through 20, adding and subtracting, and data and graphing. These pages show what I will learn and have activities for us to do together.

From, _____

Vocabulary

These are some words I will use in this unit.

addend Each of the numbers added in an addition problem

$$2 + 3 = 5$$
↑ ↑
addends

tally A mark used to record a number

graph A way to show information

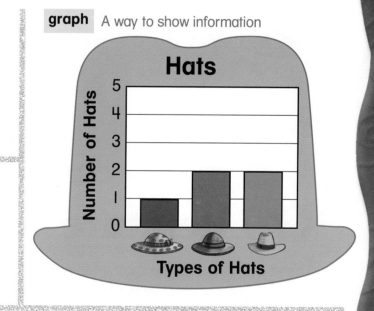

Some other words I may use are **before**, **after**, **between**, **sum**, and **difference**.

Vocabulary Activity

Let's work together to complete these sentences.

Turn the page for more.

1. A _____ is a way to show information.

2. In 4 + 2 = 6, 4 is an _____.

How To add and subtract

These addition and subtraction problems are examples of what I will be learning.

Add.

1 + 1 = ___2___

3 + 1 = ___4___

Subtract.

2 − 1 = ___1___

4 − 2 = ___2___

Literature

These books link to the math in this unit. We can look for them at the library.

Just Enough Carrots
by Stuart J. Murphy
Illustrated by
Frank Remkiewicz
(Scott Foresman, 1997)

Over in the Meadow, a Rhyme
Illustrated by Ezra Jack Keats

Let's read together!

The Best Vacation Ever
by Stuart J. Murphy

Technology

We can visit *Education Place* at

eduplace.com/parents/mw/

for the Math Lingo game, *e •* Glossary, and more games and activities to do together.

Number Concepts

CHAPTER 1

INVESTIGATION

How many red flowers are there?

Connect the Dots

Start at 1.
Finish at 10.

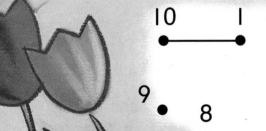

10   1   2

9   8   4   3

7   6   5

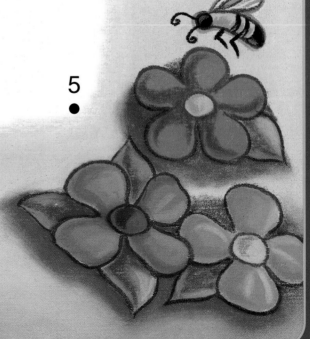

More, Fewer, and Same

MathTracks 1 / 1
Listen and Understand

Objective
Compare sets of objects.
Vocabulary
same more fewer

You can draw lines to match.

same number of hats as bows | **more** hats than bows | **fewer** hats than bows

Guided Practice

Think
I can match hats and boxes.

Match. Circle the set that has more.

1.

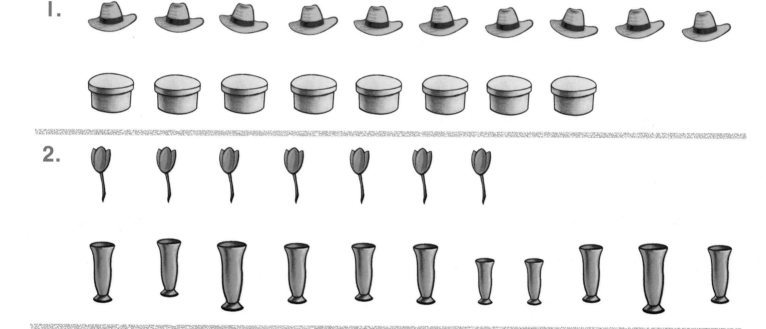

2.

3.

TEST TIPS Explain Your Thinking Tell how you could change Exercise 3 to show the same number of cups and dishes.

Match. Circle the set that has fewer.

Draw lines to match to see which set has fewer.

1.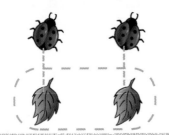

2.

3.

Draw a set that has the same number.

4.

Problem Solving ▶ Number Sense

Kwan has a set of 5 balls.

5. Draw a set with 1 more ball.

6. Draw a set with 1 fewer ball.

At Home Make small groups of plates and napkins. Ask your child to use the term **more**, **fewer**, or **same** to tell about the number of each.

Activity: Numbers 0 Through 9

MathTracks 1 / 2
Listen and Understand

Objective
Count 0 through 9 objects; read and write the numbers.

Vocabulary
number words for 0 through 9

0	1	2	3	4	5
zero	one	two	three	four	five

Work Together

Use ◯ to show the number.
Draw to show how many.

1. 3

2. 2

3. 0

4. 5

5. 4

Count.

Write the number.

1.

_____ ____ two

2.

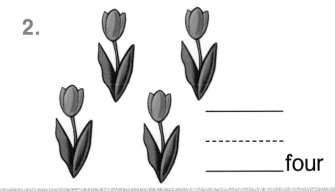

_____ ____ four

3.

_____ ____ three

4.

_____ ____ zero

5.

_____ ____ one

6.

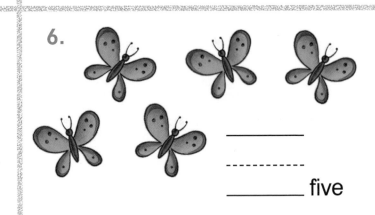

_____ ____ five

7. **Write About It** Which set has the most? _____

_____

8. Draw a set with **1** more.

Go on

6	7	8	9
six	**seven**	**eight**	**nine**

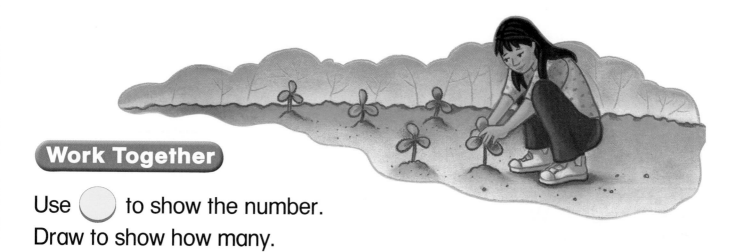

Work Together

Use ◯ to show the number.
Draw to show how many.

1. 9

2. 7

3. 6

4. 8

Count.

Write the number.

1. 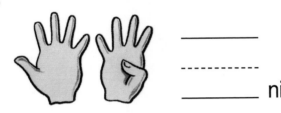 _____

_____ six

2. 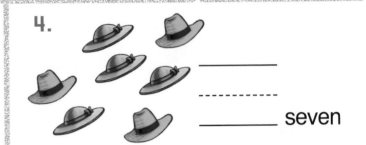 _____

_____ eight

3. _____

_____ nine

4. _____

_____ seven

5. **Talk About It** Which set has the fewest?

6. Draw a set of **9** or fewer seed packs.

7. Write the number.

_____

_____

8. Write the number word.

_____

_____

At Home Have your child count sets of 1 through 9 objects such as spoons or cereal.

Activity:
Numbers 10 Through 20

Objective
Count sets of 10 through 20 objects; read and write numbers.

Vocabulary
number words for 10 through 20

Hands-On

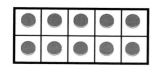

10

ten

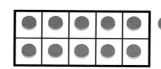

11

eleven

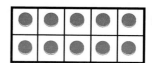

12

twelve

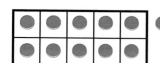

13

thirteen

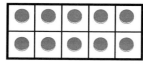 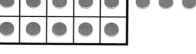

14

fourteen

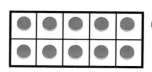

15

fifteen

Work Together

Use Workmat 1 and ⬭ to show the number.
Draw to show how many.

1. **15**

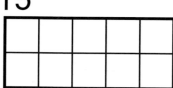

2. **12**

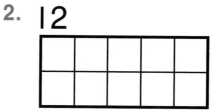

3. **14**

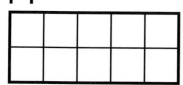

4. **11**

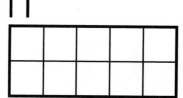

5. **10**

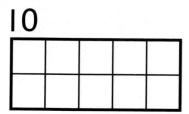

6. **13**

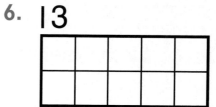

Count.

Write the number.

1.

_____ thirteen

2.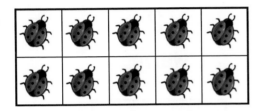

_____
- - - - - - - - - -
_____ ten

3.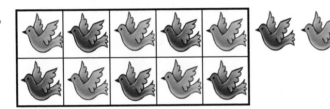

_____
- - - - - - - - - -
_____ twelve

4.

_____
- - - - - - - - - -
_____ fifteen

5.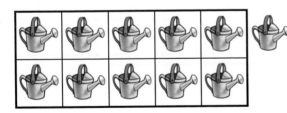

_____
- - - - - - - - - -
_____ eleven

6.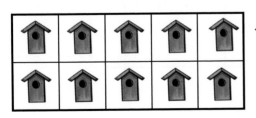

_____
- - - - - - - - - -
_____ fourteen

7. **Talk About It** Which set has the fewest?

Name ______________________________

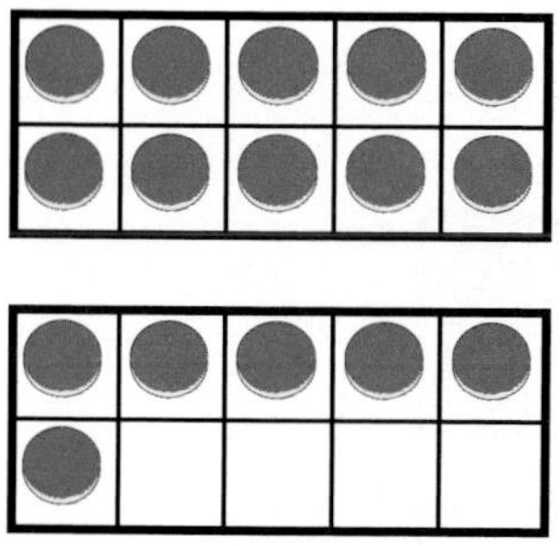

16

sixteen

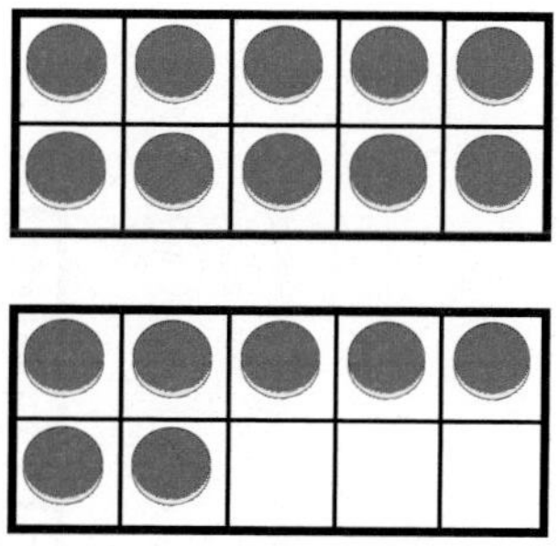

17

seventeen

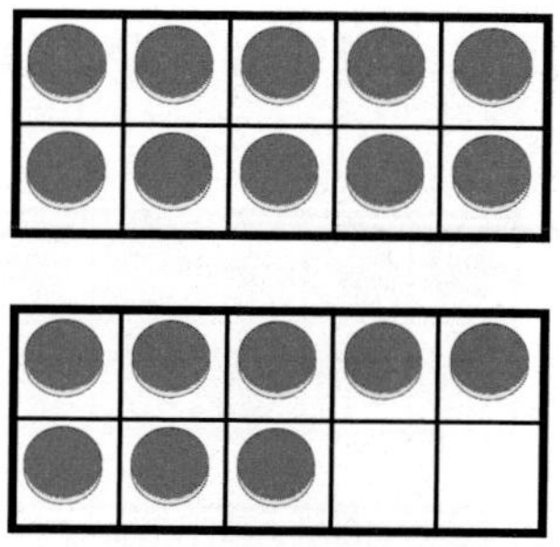

18

eighteen

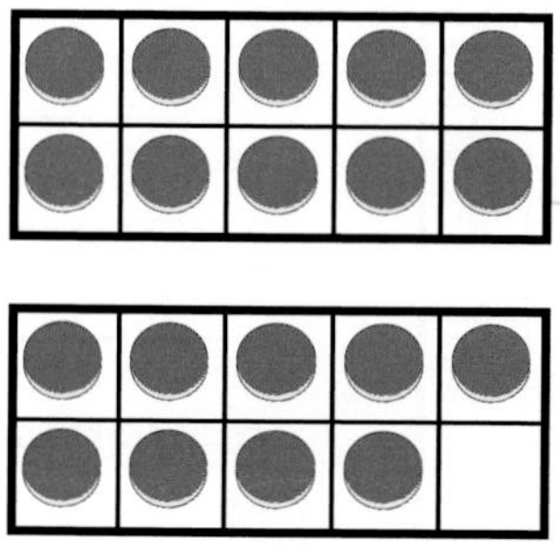

19

nineteen

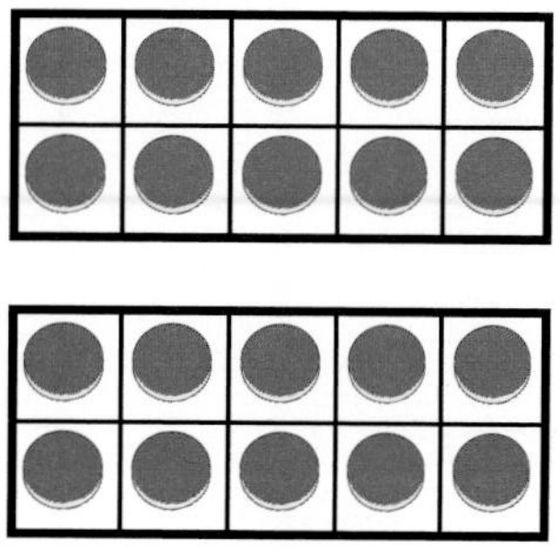

20

twenty

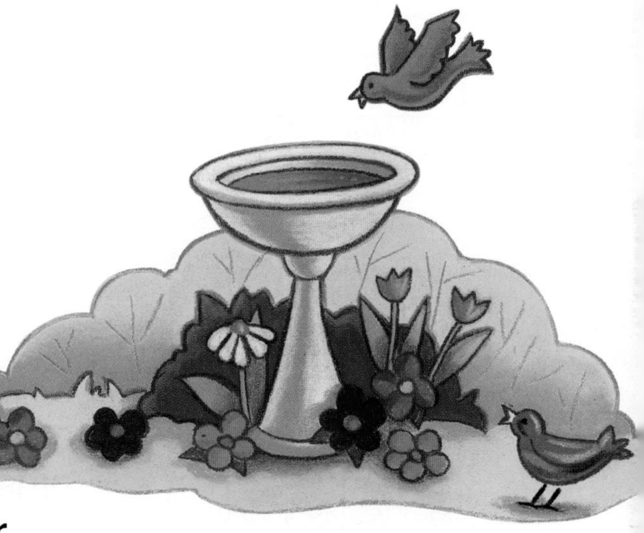

Work Together

Use Workmat 2 and 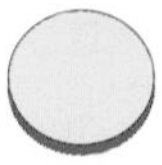 to show the number.
Draw to show how many.

1. 17

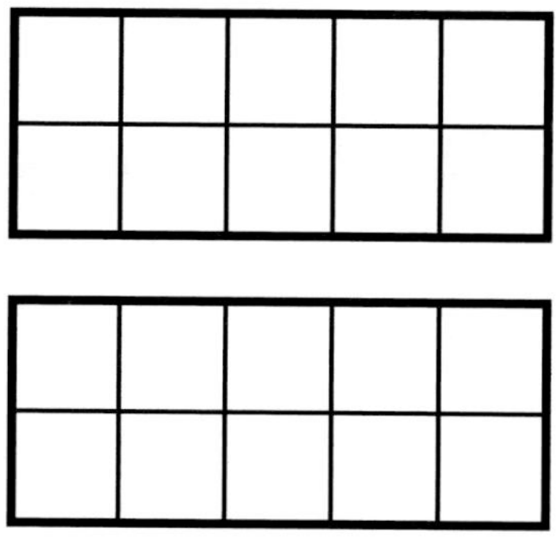

2. 20

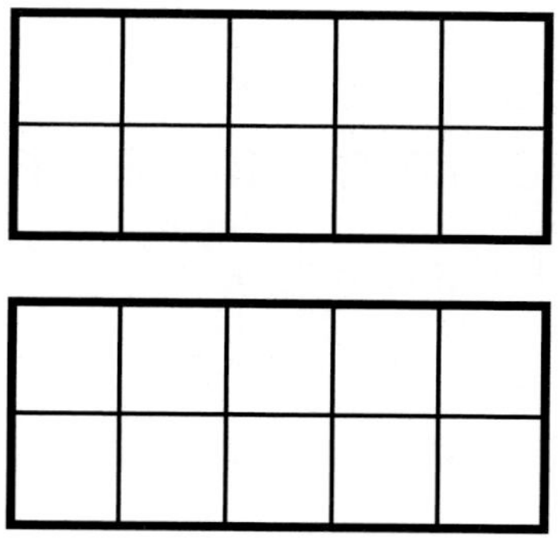

3. 19

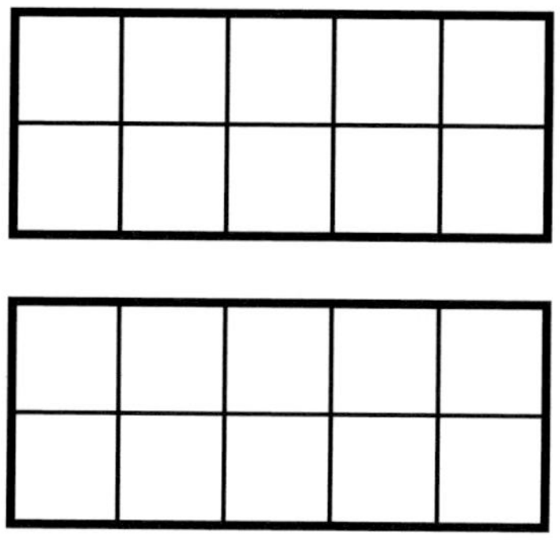

4. 18

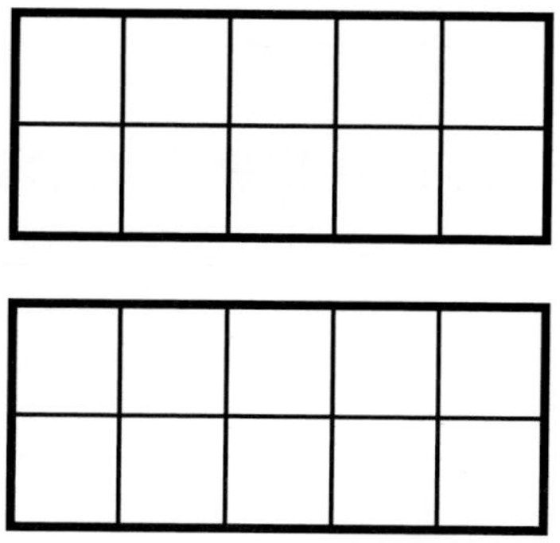

Count. Write the number.

1.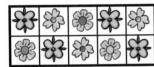
_____
- - - - - - - - - -
_____
eighteen

2.
_____
- - - - - - - - - -
_____
sixteen

3.
_____
- - - - - - - - - -
_____
twenty

4. _____
- - - - - - - - - -
_____
seventeen

5.
_____
- - - - - - - - - -
_____
nineteen

6. **Talk About It** Which set has the most?

Choose a number from
10 through **20**.

7. Write the number.
_____
- - - - - - - - - -
_____

8. Write the number word.
_____
- -
_____

9. Draw that many flowers.

16 sixteen

At Home Ask your child to count sets of up to 20 objects and write the number for each set.

Order

MathTracks 1/3
Listen and Understand

Number lines can help you put numbers in order.

6 is just **before** 7.

8 is just **after** 7.

7 is **between** 6 and 8.

0 1 2 3 4 5 6 7 8 9 10

11 is just before 12.

13 is just after 12.

12 is between 11 and 13.

11 12 13 14 15 16 17 18 19 20

Guided Practice

Write the numbers.

Think
Find 18 on the number line. Look at the number just before it.

1. Which number is just before 18? ☐

2. Which number is between 4 and 6? ☐

3. Just before

☐ , 4, 5

4. Between

0, ☐ , 2

5. Just before and just after

☐ , 14, ☐

TEST TIPS **Explain Your Thinking** Tell how to use a number line to find the number just after 19.

Practice

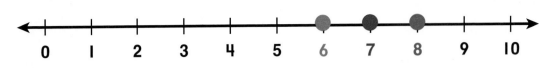

Use the number lines.

Write the numbers.

1. Just after

10, 11, [12]

3, 4, □

2. Just before

□, 8, 9

□, 18, 19

3. Between

13, □, 15

18, □, 20

4. Just before and just after

□, 1, □

□, 16, □

Problem Solving ▶ Number Sense

Write the missing number.

5. Jon has 1 more.

Max	Jon
15	

6. Ana has 1 less.

Mia	Ana
5	

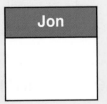 **At Home** Open a book to a page between 0 and 20. Read the page number and ask your child to identify the numbers just before and just after that number.

Go on

18 eighteen

Name _____

Now Try This Counting Forward and Backward

1. Write the missing numbers in order.

| **September** |
Sunday	Monday	Tuesday	Wednesday	Thursday	Friday	Saturday
					1	2
3						
10		12				
				21	22	23
24	25	26	27	28	29	30

Count backward. Write the numbers.

2. 20, 19, __18__, __17__, _____, _____, _____, _____,

_____, _____, __10__, _____, _____, _____, _____,

__5__, _____, _____, _____, _____

3. **Talk About It** Take turns with a classmate. Pick a number between 10 and 20. Count backward to 0 from that number.

Quick Check

Match.

1. Circle the set with more.

2. Circle the set with fewer.

Write the number.

3.

_____

_____

eight

4.

_____

_____

five

5.

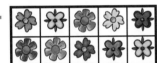

_____

_____

thirteen

6.

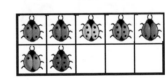

_____

_____

seventeen

11   12   13   14   15   16   17   18   19   20

7. Just after

19, ☐

8. Just before

☐, 16

9. Between

11, ☐, 13

Write the missing numbers in order.

10. 10, 11, _____, _____, 14, _____, _____, _____, 18

11. 20, 19, _____, _____, 16, _____, _____, _____, 12

Comparing Numbers

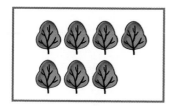 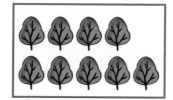

7 is **less than** 9

9 is **greater than** 8

7 is **equal to** 7

Guided Practice

Circle the words that make the sentence true.

1.

5   is greater than
    is less than   6

Think
5 dots is fewer than 6 dots. I know which number is less.

2.

10   is greater than
     is equal to   10

3.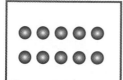

8   is greater than
    is less than   14

4. 20   is greater than
       is less than   18

5. 9   is greater than
      is less than   12

TEST TIPS **Explain Your Thinking** Read the answer to Exercise 2. What does it mean?

Count the dots to help you compare the numbers.

Circle the words that make the sentence true.

1.

6   is greater than   8
(is less than)

2.

12   is greater than   12
is equal to

3.
19   is greater than   17
is less than

4.
0   is greater than   1
is less than

5.
7   is greater than   7
is equal to

6.
14   is greater than   11
is less than

Problem Solving ▶ Number Sense

Circle the numbers greater than 6.

7.

17   10   20
4   0   14   3

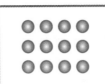 **At Home** Have your child explain how to compare two numbers using the words **greater than**, **less than**, and **equal to**.

Name_____

Greater Than, Less Than

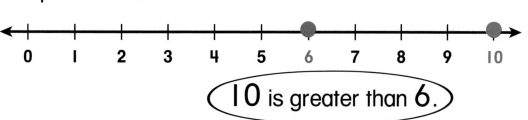 MathTracks 1/4
Listen and Understand

Compare 10 and 6.

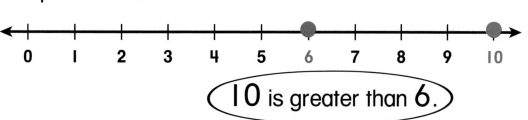

```
←──┼──┼──┼──┼──┼──┼──●──┼──┼──┼──●──→
   0  1  2  3  4  5  6  7  8  9  10
```

(10 is greater than 6.)

Compare 13 and 17.

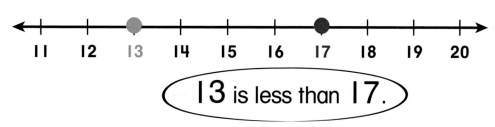

```
←──┼──┼──●──┼──┼──┼──●──┼──┼──┼──→
   11 12 13 14 15 16 17 18 19 20
```

(13 is less than 17.)

Guided Practice

Use the number lines.
Circle the greater number.

Think
6 comes after 2 on the number line.

1. 2   6

2. 4   0

3. 9   10

4. 17   11

5. 14   20

Use the number lines.
Circle the number that is less.

6. 6   7

7. 3   5

8. 5   4

9. 16   12

10. 11   15

11. 18   19

TEST TIPS **Explain Your Thinking** Which is greater, 10 or 20?
How do you know?

Find the numbers on the number line.

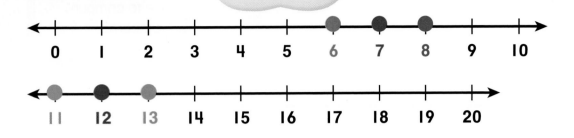

Use the number lines. Circle the greater number.

1. 14   (16)

2. 10   8

3. 15   19

4. 10   0

5. 16   17

6. 13   11

Use the number lines. Circle the number that is less.

7. 0   1

8. 18   14

9. 9   7

10. 11   12

11. 10   2

12. 16   20

Problem Solving Number Sense

13. Write two numbers that are greater than 10 but less than 20.

_____ _____

14. Write two numbers that are less than 10.

_____ _____

When you compare three or more numbers you use the words **greatest** and **least**.

15. **Write About It** Put the four numbers you wrote above in order from greatest to least.

_____ _____ _____ _____

At Home Name two numbers less than 20. Have your child tell which is greater. Repeat with two other numbers and ask your child which is less.

Name_____

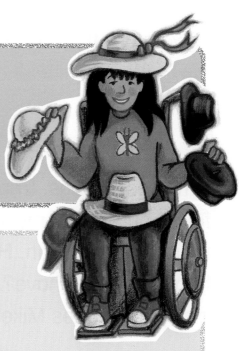

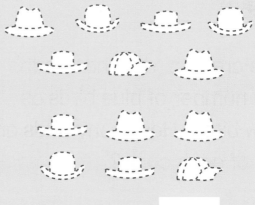

Go on ►

Name_____

Draw a Picture

Celia has 6 hats. Han has 1 more hat than Celia. Maria has 1 fewer hat than Han. How many hats does Han have? How many hats does Maria have?

UNDERSTAND

What do you know?
- Celia has 6 hats.
- Han has 1 more hat than Celia.
- Maria has 1 fewer hat than Han.

PLAN

Start with Celia's hats.

Celia has __6__ hats.

SOLVE

Draw a picture.

Draw 1 more hat to show Han's hats.

Draw 1 fewer than Han's hats to show Maria's hats.

How many hats does Han have? __7__ hats

How many hats does Maria have? __6__ hats

LOOK BACK

Does your answer make sense?

Remember:
► Understand
► Plan
► Solve
► Look Back

Draw a picture to solve.

1. There are 10 flowers. There is the same number of red flowers as orange flowers. How many flowers are there of each color?

Think
Draw 1 red flower and 1 orange flower until you have drawn 10 flowers.

_____ red

_____ orange

2. Amy has 9 bugs. Erin has 1 fewer bug than Amy. Mike has 1 more bug than Erin. How many bugs does Erin have? How many bugs does Mike have?

Think
Start with Amy's 9 bugs.

Erin has _____ bugs.

Mike has _____ bugs.

Practice

3. There are 8 birds. There is the same number of blue birds as yellow birds. How many birds are there of each color?

_____ blue

_____ yellow

4. Abby has 7 pots. Jan has 1 more pot than Abby. Luis has 1 fewer pot than Jan. How many pots does Jan have? How many pots does Luis have?

Jan has _____ pots.

Luis has _____ pots.

Go on

Name_____

Choose a Strategy

Solve.

Draw or write to explain.

1. Chi has 9 bowler hats. There is 1 more red bowler hat than green bowler hats. How many red bowler hats are there?

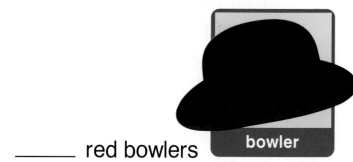

_____ red bowlers

2. The bag with the fewest yo-yos has red yo-yos in it. How many red yo-yos are there?

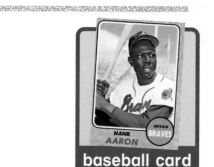

_____ red yo-yos

3. Jack has 10 baseball cards. Lee has 1 fewer. How many cards does Lee have?

_____ cards

4. Ms. Sato uses shapes to make this pattern. How many triangles has she used?

_____ triangles

 At Home Use collections to create problems that your child can solve by drawing a picture.

 **for Tests** **Listening Skills**

Listen to your teacher read the problem.
Solve.

1. There are 10 balls in a box.
   Some of the balls are red.
   6 of the balls are blue. How
   many red balls are in the box?

Show your work using pictures,
numbers, or words.

_____ red balls

2. Tad has 8 blocks in a bag.
   Ramón has 2 fewer blocks
   than Tad. How many blocks
   does Ramón have?

_____ blocks

Listen to your teacher read the problem.
Choose the correct answer.

3. 5   7   8   9
    ○   ○   ○   ○

4. 12   10   9   2
    ○   ○   ○   ○

Quick Check

Circle the words that make the sentence true.

1.

14   is greater than   10
      is less than

2.

7   is less than   7
     is equal to

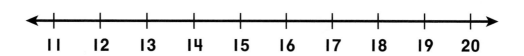

Circle the greater number.

3. 14   16   4. 17   13   5. 15   19

Circle the number that is less.

6. 11   13   7. 18   14   8. 20   17

Draw a picture to solve.

9. There are **8** buttons. There
   is the same number of red
   buttons as green buttons.
   How many are there of each?   _____ red   _____ green

Write the number.

1.

2.

3.

4.

5.

_____

6.

7.

8.

9.

10.

_____

Social Studies
Connection

Mancala

Mancala is an African game.
It is played with beads or stones.

Compare the number of beads
in each pile off the board. Circle the
words that make the sentence true.

14   is greater than
      is less than   17

12   is less than
      is equal to   12

Name_____

Vocabulary *e • Glossary*

Write the words to complete the sentence.

| greater than |
| less than |
| equal to |

1. 5 is _____ _____ 7.

2. 6 is _____ _____ 3.

Concepts and Skills

Match. Circle the set that has fewer.

3.

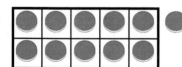

Count.
Write the number.

4. _____

5.  _____

6. _____

7. 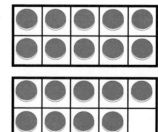 _____

8. Just after

13, ☐

9. Just before

☐, 20

10. Between

9, ☐, 11

11. Write the missing numbers in order.

11, _____, _____, 14, _____, _____, 17, _____, 19

Circle the words that make the sentence true.

12.			13.		
12	is greater than is equal to	12	5	is greater than is less than	3

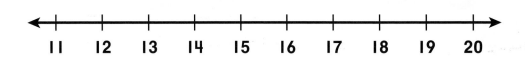

Use the number line.
Circle the greater number.

14. 11   12   15. 13   14   16. 18   15

Use the number line.
Circle the number that is less.

17. 11   13   18. 16   14   19. 17   20

Problem Solving

Draw a picture to solve.

20. There are 6 pots. There is the same number of green pots as yellow pots. How many pots are there of each color?

_____ green

_____ yellow

Addition Concepts

INVESTIGATION

How many cats and dogs do you see altogether?

Around Town

This is a parade route.

Use the parade route to answer the question.

1. How many blocks is it from the to the ?

_____ blocks

2. How many blocks is it from the  to the ?

_____ blocks

Name_____

Activity: Addition Stories

Objective
Model the concept of addition as increasing.

Work Together
Listen to the story.
Show the story with ◯ .

1.

2. **Talk About It** How do you know if your answer is correct?

On Your Own

Show the story with ◯ .
Write the numbers.

1.

___2___ girls   ___2___ boys   ___4___ in all

2.

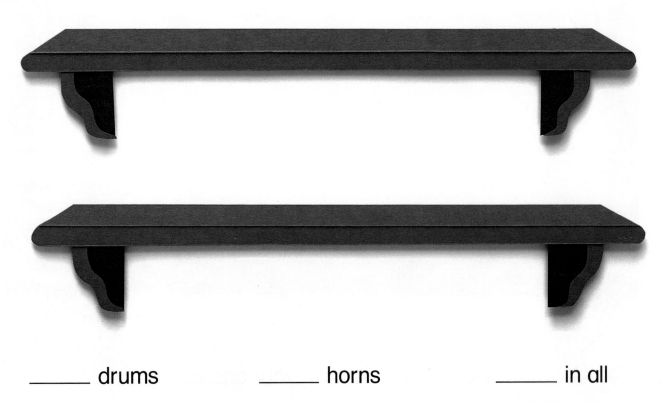

_____ drums   _____ horns   _____ in all

At Home Place a set of 2 objects and a set of 3 objects on a table.
Ask your child how many objects there are in all.

Name_____

Model Addition

💿 **MathTracks** 1/5
Listen and Understand

You **add** the **parts** to find the **whole.**

Objective
Model the concept of
addition as part-part-whole.

Vocabulary
add   part   whole

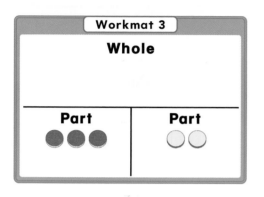

Whole	
_____	
Part	**Part**
3 ●	2 ○

Whole	
5	
Part	**Part**
3 ●	2 ○

Guided Practice

Use Workmat 3 and ○ .
Show the parts. Find the whole.

1.

Whole	
_____	
Part	**Part**
1 ●	3 ○

Think
I add 1 and 3
to find the whole.

2.

Whole	
_____	
Part	**Part**
2 ●	3 ○

TEST TIPS **Explain Your Thinking** What does the word **add** mean?

Add the parts to find how many in all.

Use Workmat 3 and ◯.
Show the parts. Find the whole.

1.

Whole
3

Part	Part
1 ●	2 ○

2.

Whole
___

Part	Part
2 ●	3 ○

3.

Whole
___

Part	Part
3 ●	1 ○

4.

Whole
___

Part	Part
3 ●	2 ○

5.

Whole
___

Part	Part
2 ●	2 ○

6.

Whole
___

Part	Part
1 ●	4 ○

Problem Solving ▶ Number Sense

Write the parts.
Write the whole.

7.

Whole
___

Part	Part
___ ●	___ ○

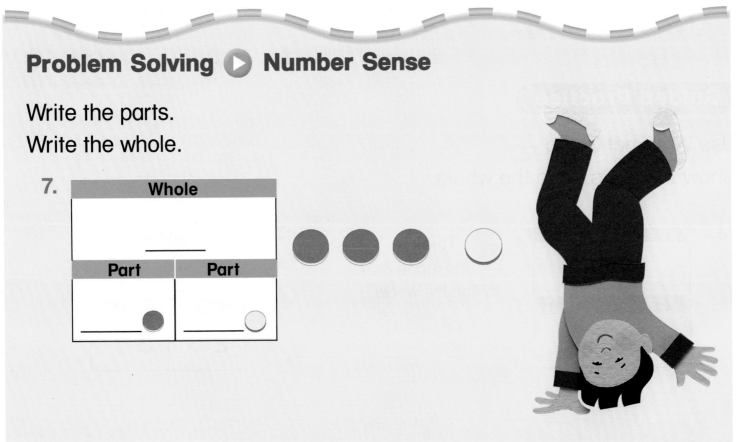

At Home Use dried beans or other objects to help your child model different ways to show 5 in all.

Use Symbols to Add

MathTracks 1/6
Listen and Understand

Use the **plus sign** and **equal sign** to write an **addition sentence.**

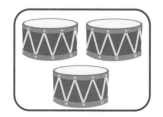

$$3 \quad + \quad 1 \quad = \quad \underline{\quad} \quad \leftarrow \quad \textbf{sum}$$

plus sign   equal sign

The sum tells how many in all.

Think
I need to add the parts.

Guided Practice

Write the sum.

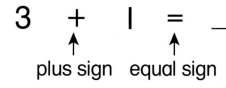

1. 

$$2 \quad + \quad 4 \quad = \quad \underline{\quad}$$

2.

$$1 \quad + \quad 5 \quad = \quad \underline{\quad}$$

3.

$$3 \quad + \quad 2 \quad = \quad \underline{\quad}$$

4.

$$3 \quad + \quad 3 \quad = \quad \underline{\quad}$$

5.

$$1 \quad + \quad 3 \quad = \quad \underline{\quad}$$

6.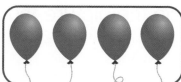

$$1 \quad + \quad 4 \quad = \quad \underline{\quad}$$

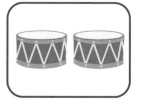

TEST TIPS **Explain Your Thinking** When you find the sum, are you finding the parts or the whole? Tell how you know.

Find the sum by putting the objects together.

Write the sum.

1.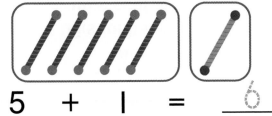

   5 + 1 = __6__

2.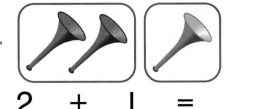

   2 + 1 = _____

3.

   2 + 2 = _____

4.

   2 + 3 = _____

5.

   4 + 2 = _____

6.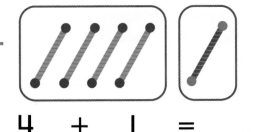

   4 + 1 = _____

7.

   1 + 1 = _____

8.

   1 + 2 = _____

Problem Solving ▶ Visual Thinking

9. Circle the picture that shows 1 + 4 = 5.

At Home Have your child cut out pictures from magazines and paste them onto blank paper to create addition stories with sums of 6 or less.

Add With Zero

When you add **zero** to a number, the sum is the number.

Objective
Solve addition problems with zero.
Vocabulary
zero

There are 4 drums.
There are none added.

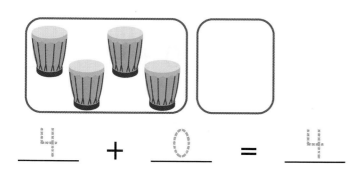

___4___ + ___0___ = ___4___

There are still 4 drums.

There are no drums.
3 drums are added.

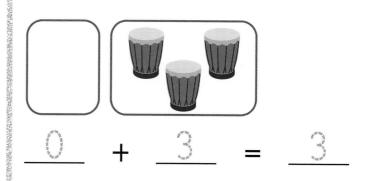

___0___ + ___3___ = ___3___

There are 3 drums.

Guided Practice

Write the sum.

Think
There is 1 flag.
None are added.

1.

___ + ___ = ___

2.

___ + ___ = ___

3. $3 + 0 = $ ____   4. $0 + 2 = $ ____   5. $6 + 0 = $ ____

TEST TIPS **Explain Your Thinking** When you add zero, you can say you added none. What other words can you use for zero?

Remember adding zero
means you add none.

Write the sum.

1.

    3 + 0 = _3_

2.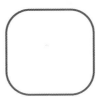

    0 + 2 = ___

3. 4 + 0 = ___   4. 2 + 3 = ___   5. 0 + 4 = ___

6. 2 + 1 = ___   7. 5 + 0 = ___   8. 3 + 3 = ___

9. 2 + 4 = ___   10. 0 + 6 = ___   11. 1 + 4 = ___

12. 0 + 1 = ___   13. 2 + 2 = ___   14. 5 + 1 = ___

15. 3 + 1 = ___   16. 4 + 2 = ___   17. 0 + 0 = ___

18. 1 + 1 = ___   19. 2 + 0 = ___   20. 3 + 2 = ___

Reading Math ▶ Vocabulary

Write the addition sentence.

21. Four plus two equals six.   ___ ◯ ___ ◯ ___

22. Three plus zero equals three.   ___ ◯ ___ ◯ ___

At Home Ask your child to explain what
happens when you add zero to a number.

Go on ▶

Writing Math: Create and Solve

Write an addition story about the children above.
Complete the addition sentence.

1. _____

   _____

   _____

2. _____ + _____ = _____ children

Write a story to match the number sentence. $3 + 3 = 6$

3. _____

   _____

   _____

Draw a picture to show your story.

4.

Quick Check

Show the story with  .
Write the numbers.

1.

_____ cat   _____ dogs   _____ in all

Use Workmat 3 and ⬤ .
Show the parts. Find the whole.

2.

Whole
_____

Part	Part
4 ⬤	1 ◯

3.

Whole
_____

Part	Part
3 ⬤	1 ◯

Write the sum.

4.

2 + 3 = _____

5.

1 + 2 = _____

6. 3 + 0 = _____   7. 0 + 0 = _____   8. 0 + 6 = _____

9. 2 + 2 = _____   10. 4 + 2 = _____   11. 5 + 0 = _____

Name_____

Add in Any Order

You can change the **order** of the **addends** and get the same sum.

Hands-On

Objective
Understand the order property of addition.

Vocabulary
order   addend

Make a cube train.

___4___ + ___1___ = ___5___

Turn it around.

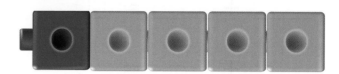

___1___ + ___4___ = ___5___

Guided Practice

Use cubes in two colors. Make the train.
Complete the two addition sentences for the train.

1. Make a **3** train.

___2___ + ___1___ = ___3___

____ + ____ = ____

Think
2 plus 1 equals 3.
I change the order of the addends to complete the sentence.

2. Make a **6** train.

____ + ____ = ____

____ + ____ = ____

3. Make a **4** train.

____ + ____ = ____

____ + ____ = ____

TEST TIPS **Explain Your Thinking** Why is the sum of **5 + 1** the same as **1 + 5**?

Remember to turn your train around.

Use cubes in two colors. Make the train.
Complete the two addition sentences for the train.

1. Make a 6 train.

$$\underline{5} + \underline{1} = \underline{6}$$

$$\underline{1} + \underline{5} = \underline{6}$$

2. Make a 5 train.

$$\underline{} + \underline{} = \underline{}$$

$$\underline{} + \underline{} = \underline{}$$

Add. Then change the order and complete
a new addition sentence.

3. $2 + 3 = \underline{}$

$$\underline{} + \underline{} = \underline{}$$

4. $5 + 0 = \underline{}$

$$\underline{} + \underline{} = \underline{}$$

5. $0 + 3 = \underline{}$

$$\underline{} + \underline{} = \underline{}$$

6. $3 + 3 = \underline{}$

$$\underline{} + \underline{} = \underline{}$$

Algebra Readiness ▶ Functions

Use the rule. Write the sum.

7.

Add 1	
2	3
3	4
4	
5	

8.

Add 2	
2	4
3	5
4	
5	

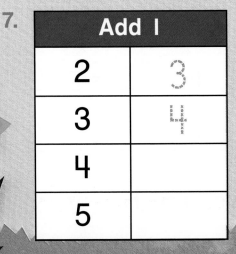

At Home Write one of the addition sentences that appear on this page.
Have your child change the order and write a new addition sentence. Repeat.

Name_____

Ways to Make 7 and 8

Objective
Complete addition sentences with sums of 7 and 8 using two addends.

There are different ways to make a number.

Here are two ways to make **7**.

_6_ + _1_ = _7_

_4_ + _3_ = _7_

Here are two ways to make **8**.

_1_ + _7_ = _8_

_2_ + _6_ = _8_

Guided Practice

Use two colors to show another way to make **7**.
Complete the addition sentence.

Think
I can use 5 blue cubes and 2 red cubes.

1. ⬜⬜⬜⬜⬜⬜⬜

_5_ + _2_ = _7_

Use two colors to show another way to make **8**.
Complete the addition sentence.

2. ⬜⬜⬜⬜⬜⬜⬜⬜

____ + ____ = ____

TEST TIPS **Explain Your Thinking** Look at the sentence in Exercise 1.
Explain why you get the same sum if you add **2 + 5**.

Remember there are many ways to make a sum.

Use two colors to show a way to make **7**.

Complete the addition sentence.

1. ☐☐☐☐☐☐☐ $\underline{3}$ + $\underline{4}$ = $\underline{7}$

2. ☐☐☐☐☐☐☐   _____ + _____ = _____

Use two colors to show a way to make **8**.

Complete the addition sentence.

3. ☐☐☐☐☐☐☐☐   _____ + _____ = _____

4. ☐☐☐☐☐☐☐☐   _____ + _____ = _____

Write the sum.

5. $5 + 2 =$ _____   6. $4 + 1 =$ _____   7. $2 + 2 =$ _____

8. $2 + 0 =$ _____   9. $6 + 1 =$ _____   10. $3 + 2 =$ _____

Algebra Readiness ▶ Properties

Use cubes. Write the missing number.

11. $2 + 1 = 1 +$ ☐   12. $3 + 2 =$ ☐ $+ 3$

13. $4 +$ ☐ $= 2 + 4$ 14. ☐ $+ 5 = 5 + 2$

🏠 **At Home** Have your child tell addition stories with sums of 7 or 8.

Add in Vertical Form

 MathTracks 1/7
Listen and Understand

You can write the same addition fact in two ways.

Add across.

Add down.

The sum is the same.

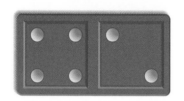

$$\underline{4} + \underline{2} = \underline{6}$$

 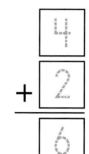

Guided Practice

Complete the addition fact.

1.

 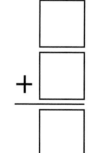

____ + ____ = ____

Think
The number of dots is the same, so the sum is the same.

2.

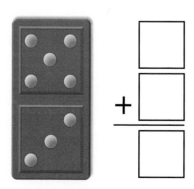

____ + ____ = ____

TEST TIPS **Explain Your Thinking** Write $6 + 1$ in two ways.

Why is the sum the same?

Remember to add to find how many dots in all.

Complete the addition fact.

1.
   $\begin{array}{r} 5 \\ + 2 \\ \hline 7 \end{array}$

2.
   $\begin{array}{r} \square \\ + \square \\ \hline \square \end{array}$

3.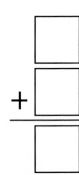
   $\begin{array}{r} \square \\ + \square \\ \hline \square \end{array}$

4.
   $\begin{array}{r} \square \\ + \square \\ \hline \square \end{array}$

___ + ___ = ___

Write the sum.

5. $\begin{array}{r} 2 \\ +2 \\ \hline \end{array}$
6. $\begin{array}{r} 1 \\ +4 \\ \hline \end{array}$
7. $\begin{array}{r} 4 \\ +4 \\ \hline \end{array}$
8. $\begin{array}{r} 2 \\ +5 \\ \hline \end{array}$
9. $\begin{array}{r} 3 \\ +3 \\ \hline \end{array}$
10. $\begin{array}{r} 4 \\ +0 \\ \hline \end{array}$

11. $\begin{array}{r} 1 \\ +5 \\ \hline \end{array}$
12. $\begin{array}{r} 4 \\ +3 \\ \hline \end{array}$
13. $\begin{array}{r} 3 \\ +2 \\ \hline \end{array}$
14. $\begin{array}{r} 8 \\ +0 \\ \hline \end{array}$
15. $\begin{array}{r} 3 \\ +5 \\ \hline \end{array}$
16. $\begin{array}{r} 7 \\ +0 \\ \hline \end{array}$

Algebra Readiness ▶ Patterns

Write the sums. Look for a pattern.
Write the addition fact you think will come next.

17. $\begin{array}{r} 1 \\ +2 \\ \hline \square \end{array}$
    $\begin{array}{r} 2 \\ +2 \\ \hline \square \end{array}$
    $\begin{array}{r} 3 \\ +2 \\ \hline \square \end{array}$
    $\begin{array}{r} 4 \\ +2 \\ \hline \square \end{array}$
    $\begin{array}{r} \square \\ + \square \\ \hline \square \end{array}$

 At Home Show a group of 3 objects and a group of 4 objects. Ask your child to write an addition fact across and down about the groups.

Write a Number Sentence

Objective
Write addition sentences to solve story problems.

How many children in all?

UNDERSTAND

What do you know?

· There are **2** children in a group.
· **3** more children join them.

PLAN

Circle how you would solve the problem. (add)   subtract

SOLVE

Write an addition sentence.

2 (+) 3 (=) 5

How many children in all?   ____5____ children

LOOK BACK

Does the addition sentence show the two groups?
Does the sum show how many in all?

Write an addition sentence to solve.
Write the answer.

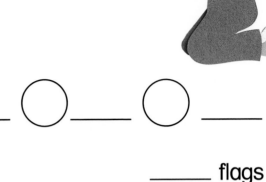

1. There are **6** red flags. There are **2** blue flags. How many flags are there?

Think
6 in one group.
2 in the other.

____ ◯ ____ ◯ ____

_____ flags

2. There are **4** children. Then **3** more children come. How many children are there now?

Think
4 children and
3 more children.

____ ◯ ____ ◯ ____

_____ children

3. There are **5** cats. Then **I** cat joins them. How many cats are there now?

____ ◯ ____ ◯ ____

_____ cats

4. There are **3** blue drums. There are **5** green drums. How many drums in all?

____ ◯ ____ ◯ ____

_____ drums

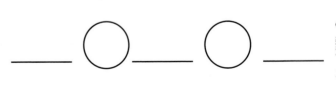

Go on

Name_____

Choose a Strategy

Solve.

1. There are 2 girls playing the clarinet. There are 5 boys playing the clarinet. How many children are playing the clarinet?

   Draw or write to explain.

   clarinet

   _____ children

2. There are 5 oboes on the top shelf. There is 1 more oboe on the bottom shelf than on the top shelf. How many oboes are on the bottom shelf?

   oboe

   _____ oboes

3. There are 6 flute players. 2 more flute players join them. Now how many flute players are there?

   flute

   _____ flute players

4. **Multistep** There are 5 trumpet players. 1 more trumpet player joins them. Then, 1 trumpet player leaves. How many trumpet players are there now?

   trumpet

   _____ trumpet players

At Home Read problems 1 through 4 using different numbers or objects and have your child tell how to solve the problems.

Listen to your teacher read the problem.
Solve.

1. Arlo sees 2 dogs in the park. How many dog legs does he see?	Show your work using pictures, numbers, or words. _____ legs
2. Sasha has 3 books. She gets 2 more books. How many books does Sasha have now?	 _____ books

Listen to your teacher read the problem.
Choose the correct answer.

3. 4   5   7   8
    ○   ○   ○   ○

4. 3   5   6   7
    ○   ○   ○   ○

Name_____

Add. Then change the order and complete
a new addition sentence.

1.   3 + 2 = ____

   ____ + ____ = ____

2.   1 + 5 = ____

   ____ + ____ = ____

Write the sum.

3. 4 + 4 = ____

4. 5 + 2 = ____

5. 7 + 1 = ____

6. 0 + 7 = ____

7. 3 + 4 = ____

8. 8 + 0 = ____

9.   3
    +1
   ____

10.   0
    +5
   ____

11.   6
    +2
   ____

12.   1
    +6
   ____

13.   3
    +3
   ____

14.   2
    +4
   ____

Write an addition sentence
to solve.

15. There are 2 red
    balloons. There are
    5 yellow balloons.
    How many balloons
    are there?

____ balloons

Write the number.

1.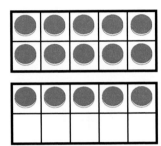

    _____

2.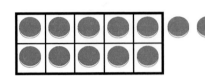

    _____

3.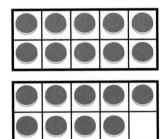

    _____

4.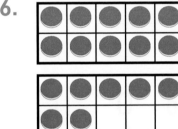

    _____

5.

    _____

6.

    _____

Math Challenge

CRAB LEGS

A crab has **5** pairs of legs. It uses **3** pairs of legs to walk. It uses **1** pair of legs to swim. The last pair of legs has large claws. How many legs does a crab have?

_____ legs

Name_____

Vocabulary (*e* • Glossary)

Write a word to complete the sentence.

add	
sum	
plus	

1. The _____ tells how many in all.

2. The _____ sign means add.

Concepts and Skills

Listen to the story.
Draw counters to show the story.
Write the numbers.

3.

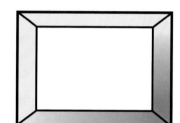

_____    _____ ◯   _____ in all

Write how many in all.

4.

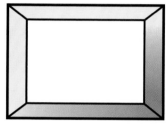

Whole
_____

Part	Part
4 ●	1 ◯

5.

Whole
_____

Part	Part
1 ●	2 ◯

6.

2 + 2 = _____

7.

3 + 1 = _____

Write the sum.

8. $2 + 0 = $ _____　　9. $0 + 0 = $ _____　　10. $0 + 5 = $ _____

Add. Then change the order and complete
a new addition sentence.

11. 　$4 \;+\; 1 \;=$ _____　　　12. 　$2 \;+\; 4 \;=$ _____

　　_____ $+$ _____ $=$ _____　　　　　_____ $+$ _____ $=$ _____

Write the sum.

13. $3 + 3 = $ _____　　14. $5 + 3 = $ _____　　15. $2 + 5 = $ _____

16. $0 + 6 = $ _____　　17. $4 + 3 = $ _____　　18. $2 + 6 = $ _____

19. $\begin{array}{r} 1 \\ +3 \\ \hline \end{array}$ 　　20. $\begin{array}{r} 6 \\ +0 \\ \hline \end{array}$ 　　21. $\begin{array}{r} 2 \\ +2 \\ \hline \end{array}$ 　　22. $\begin{array}{r} 6 \\ +1 \\ \hline \end{array}$ 　　23. $\begin{array}{r} 4 \\ +4 \\ \hline \end{array}$ 　　24. $\begin{array}{r} 0 \\ +8 \\ \hline \end{array}$

Problem Solving

Write an addition sentence to solve.
Write the answer.

25. There are 3 red balloons.
　　There are 4 yellow balloons.
　　How many balloons in all?

_____ $\bigcirc$ _____ $\bigcirc$ _____

_____ balloons

Subtraction Concepts

CHAPTER 3

INVESTIGATION

When the pig takes the pumpkin,
how many pumpkins will be left?

Harvest Time

Listen to your teacher.

Activity: Subtraction Stories

Objective
Model subtraction stories.

Work Together

Listen to the story.
Show the story with  .

I.

2. **Talk About It** Tell how showing subtraction with
counters is different from showing addition.

Listen for the number that tells how many in all.

Listen to the story.
Show the story with  .
Write the numbers.

1.

____4____ 🍎   ____2____ picked   ____2____ left

2.

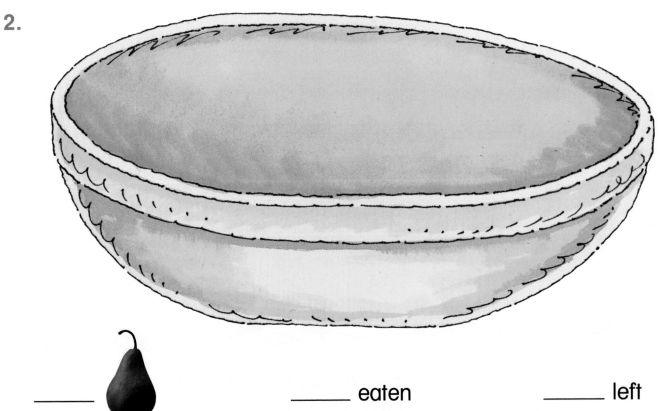

____ 🍐   ____ eaten   ____ left

At Home Ask your child to use objects and create a story about subtracting.

Name_____

Model Subtraction

MathTracks 1 / 8
Listen to Understand

If you know the **whole** and one of the **parts,**
you can **subtract** to find the other part.

Objective
Model the concept of subtraction with parts and wholes.

Vocabulary
whole   part   subtract

There are 4 counters in all.
3 counters are red.
How many are yellow?

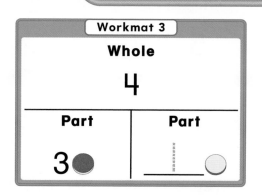

There is 1 yellow counter.

Guided Practice

Use Workmat 3 and ◯ .
Show the red part. Find the yellow part.
Write how many yellow.

1.
Whole	
3	
Part	Part
2●	____◯

Think
There are 3 counters in all. One part has 2 counters.

2.
Whole	
4	
Part	Part
2●	____◯

3.
Whole	
5	
Part	Part
4●	____◯

4.
Whole	
2	
Part	Part
1●	____◯

5.
Whole	
4	
Part	Part
1●	____◯

TEST TIPS **Explain Your Thinking** If you have 4 in all and 1
is red, can you have more than 3 yellow? Why?

Practice

The parts make the whole.

Use Workmat 3 and .
Show the red part. Find the yellow part.
Write how many yellow.

1.

Whole	
5	
Part	**Part**
1	4 ___

2.

Whole	
3	
Part	**Part**
2●	___

3.

Whole	
4	
Part	**Part**
3●	___

4.

Whole	
5	
Part	**Part**
3●	___

5.

Whole	
5	
Part	**Part**
4●	___

6.

Whole	
2	
Part	**Part**
1●	___

Problem Solving ▶ Number Sense

Draw a set with 1 fewer.

7.

8.

9. Talk About It How do you know there is 1 fewer object?

At Home Start with a set of 5 objects. Move some to the left to show one part. Have your child tell how many are in the other part.

64 sixty-four

Use Symbols to Subtract

 **MathTracks** 1/9
Listen to Understand

Use the **minus sign** and **equal sign** to write about subtraction.

Objective
Solve subtraction sentences using − and =.
Vocabulary
minus sign
equal sign

$6 - 2 = $ ____

↑   ↑
minus sign   equal sign

You can circle and cross out to show subtraction.

Guided Practice

Circle and cross out to subtract.
Write how many are left.

1.

    $5 - 3 = $ ____

Think
Circle 3 and cross them out.

2.

    $4 - 1 = $ ____

3.

    $6 - 5 = $ ____

4.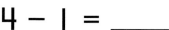

    $6 - 3 = $ ____

5.

    $5 - 2 = $ ____

TEST TIPS **Explain Your Thinking** In Exercise 5, why do you circle two objects before you subtract?

Circle and cross out to subtract.
Write how many are left.

1.

6 – 1 = ___5___

2.

5 – 2 = _____

3.

4 – 3 = _____

4.

3 – 1 = _____

5.

6 – 3 = _____

6.

4 – 2 = _____

7.

3 – 2 = _____

8.

6 – 4 = _____

Problem Solving ▶ Visual Thinking

Circle the picture that shows 5 – 4 = 1.

9.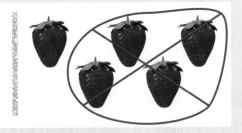

 At Home Draw 5 or 6 objects. Have your child circle and cross out some and then write how many are left.

Name_____

Write Subtraction Sentences

Write a **subtraction sentence** to find how many are left.

__6__ – __4__ = __2__

↑
difference

The **difference** in this subtraction sentence tells how many are left.

There are 6 seed packs. A rabbit takes 4 of them. 2 seed packs are left.

Guided Practice

Tell a story.
Write the subtraction sentence.

1.

____ ◯ ____ ◯ ____

2.

____ ◯ ____ ◯ ____

3.

____ ◯ ____ ◯ ____

4.

____ ◯ ____ ◯ ____

TEST TIPS **Explain Your Thinking** What does the difference mean in these subtraction sentences?

Write the subtraction sentence.

1.

_3_ ◯ _1_ ◯ _2_

2.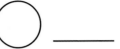

___ ◯ ___ ◯ ___

3.

___ ◯ ___ ◯ ___

4.

___ ◯ ___ ◯ ___

Write the difference.

5. $5 - 3 =$ _____

6. $2 - 1 =$ _____

7. $4 - 3 =$ _____

8. $3 - 2 =$ _____

9. $6 - 1 =$ _____

10. $5 - 4 =$ _____

11. $4 - 1 =$ _____

12. $6 - 5 =$ _____

13. $5 - 2 =$ _____

Problem Solving ▶ Logical Thinking

14. I am greater than 4.
    I am less than 7.
    I am not 5.
    What number am I?

Draw or write to explain.

_____

At Home Use objects to act out a subtraction story. Have your child write a subtraction sentence for the story. Repeat with different stories.

Go on ▶

Writing Math: Create and Solve

Write a subtraction story about the bees.
Complete the subtraction sentence.

1. _____

_____

_____

2. ____ ◯ ____ ◯ ____ bees left

Write a story to match the number sentence. 4 − 1 = 3

3. _____

_____

_____

Draw a picture to show your story.

4.

Quick Check

Listen to the story.
Draw counters to show the story.
Write the numbers.

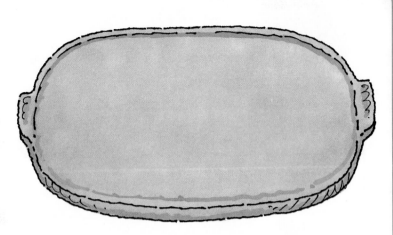

1.

 _____   _____ eaten   _____ left

Use Workmat 3 and .
Show the red part. Find the yellow part.
Write how many yellow.

2.

Whole	
5	
Part	**Part**
1 ●	_____ ○

3.

Whole	
6	
Part	**Part**
4 ●	_____ ○

Circle and cross out to subtract.
Write how many are left.

4.

$6 - 3 =$ _____

5.

$5 - 2 =$ _____

Write the difference.

6. $4 - 3 =$ _____   7. $3 - 2 =$ _____   8. $5 - 3 =$ _____

9. $6 - 1 =$ _____   10. $2 - 1 =$ _____   11. $4 - 2 =$ _____

Name_____

Zero in Subtraction

When you subtract ⬚ zero ⬚ from a number, you get the number.

__6__ – __0__ = __6__

When you subtract a number from itself, you get zero.

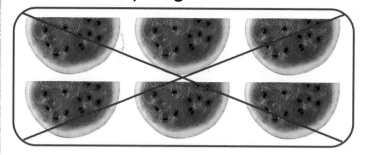

__6__ – __6__ = __0__

Think
None are crossed out.

Guided Practice

Write the difference.

1.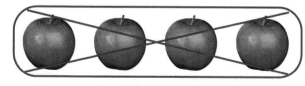

    5 – 0 = ____

2.

    5 – 5 = ____

3.

    4 – 4 = ____

4.

    4 – 0 = ____

5.

    3 – 3 = ____

6.

    3 – 0 = ____

TEST TIPS **Explain Your Thinking** When do you get a difference of zero?

Take away all and zero is left.
Take away zero and all is left.

Write the difference.

1.

$2 - 0 = \underline{2}$

2.

$4 - 0 = \underline{}$

3.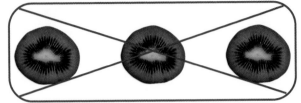

$3 - 3 = \underline{}$

4.

$4 - 4 = \underline{}$

5. $6 - 0 = \underline{}$

6. $1 - 1 = \underline{}$

7. $5 - 5 = \underline{}$

8. $2 - 0 = \underline{}$

9. $6 - 6 = \underline{}$

10. $3 - 0 = \underline{}$

11. $2 - 2 = \underline{}$

12. $5 - 0 = \underline{}$

13. $1 - 0 = \underline{}$

Reading Math ▶ Vocabulary

Write the subtraction sentence.

14. Six minus four equals two.

_____ ◯ _____ ◯ _____

15. Five minus five equals zero.

_____ ◯ _____ ◯ _____

 **At Home** Ask your child to show how $4 - 4$ and $4 - 0$ are different.

Name_____

Subtract From 8 or Less

Objective
Subtract from 8 or less and write subtraction sentences.

Use 7 cubes.
Circle and cross out 2.
Write the subtraction sentence.

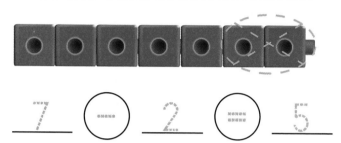

7 ◯ 2 ◯ 5

Use 8 cubes.
Circle and cross out 1.
Write the subtraction sentence.

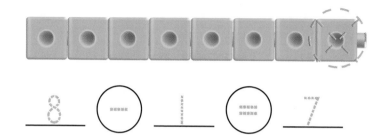

8 ◯ 1 ◯ 7

Guided Practice

Use cubes. Snap off some.
Circle and cross out.
Write the subtraction sentence.

Use 7 cubes.

Think
I can snap off 1 cube and find the difference.

1.    7 ◯ 1 ◯ 6

2. ____ ◯ ____ ◯ ____

Use 8 cubes.

3.    ____ ◯ ____ ◯ ____

4. 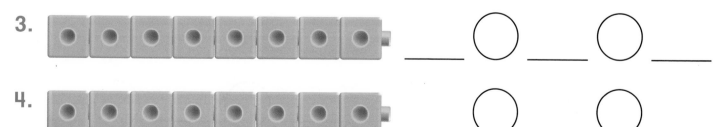   ____ ◯ ____ ◯ ____

TEST TIPS **Explain Your Thinking** What are all the ways to subtract from 7? What about 8?

Use cubes. Snap off some.

Circle and cross out.

Write the subtraction sentence.

Use **7** cubes.

1.  $\underline{7}\ \bigcirc\ \underline{4}\ \bigcirc\ \underline{3}$

2.  $\underline{}\ \bigcirc\ \underline{}\ \bigcirc\ \underline{}$

Use **8** cubes.

3.  $\underline{}\ \bigcirc\ \underline{}\ \bigcirc\ \underline{}$

4.  $\underline{}\ \bigcirc\ \underline{}\ \bigcirc\ \underline{}$

Write the difference.

5. $7 - 0 = \underline{}$ 6. $8 - 1 = \underline{}$ 7. $7 - 6 = \underline{}$

8. $8 - 6 = \underline{}$ 9. $7 - 7 = \underline{}$ 10. $8 - 0 = \underline{}$

Algebra Readiness ▶ Number Sentences

Write the subtraction sentence.

11. Pat has **7** apples.
    He eats **2** of them.
    How many apples are left?

$\underline{}\ \bigcirc\ \underline{}\ \bigcirc\ \underline{}$

12. **Talk About It** What do the numbers in the subtraction sentence stand for?

 **At Home** Show 8 or fewer objects. Take some away. Ask your child to write the subtraction sentence.

Subtract in Vertical Form

 MathTracks 1 / 10
Listen to Understand

You can write the same subtraction fact in two ways.

Subtract across.

Subtract down.

The difference is the same.

$8 - 3 = 5$ ← difference

5 ← difference

Guided Practice

Complete the subtraction fact.

1.

Think
I write 5 in the first space. I write 1 after the minus sign.

____ − ____ = ____

2.

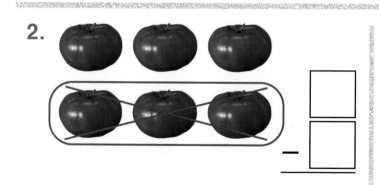

____ − ____ = ____

3.

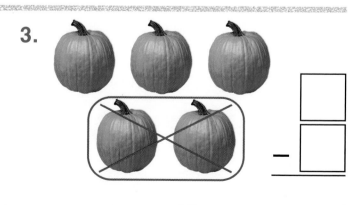

____ − ____ = ____

TEST TIPS **Explain Your Thinking** Whether you subtract across or subtract down, the difference is the same. Why?

Remember to write the number you start with in the first space.

Complete the subtraction fact.

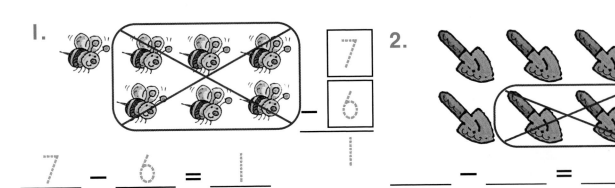

1. $\begin{array}{r} 7 \\ -6 \\ \hline 1 \end{array}$

$7 - 6 = 1$

2. $\begin{array}{r} \\ - \\ \hline \end{array}$

$\underline{} - \underline{} = \underline{}$

Write the difference.

3. $\begin{array}{r} 8 \\ -0 \\ \hline \end{array}$
4. $\begin{array}{r} 7 \\ -2 \\ \hline \end{array}$
5. $\begin{array}{r} 4 \\ -4 \\ \hline \end{array}$
6. $\begin{array}{r} 8 \\ -1 \\ \hline \end{array}$
7. $\begin{array}{r} 6 \\ -5 \\ \hline \end{array}$
8. $\begin{array}{r} 5 \\ -4 \\ \hline \end{array}$

9. $\begin{array}{r} 6 \\ -0 \\ \hline \end{array}$
10. $\begin{array}{r} 7 \\ -4 \\ \hline \end{array}$
11. $\begin{array}{r} 8 \\ -7 \\ \hline \end{array}$
12. $\begin{array}{r} 8 \\ -5 \\ \hline \end{array}$
13. $\begin{array}{r} 4 \\ -3 \\ \hline \end{array}$
14. $\begin{array}{r} 6 \\ -6 \\ \hline \end{array}$

15. $\begin{array}{r} 8 \\ -3 \\ \hline \end{array}$
16. $\begin{array}{r} 6 \\ -3 \\ \hline \end{array}$
17. $\begin{array}{r} 8 \\ -8 \\ \hline \end{array}$
18. $\begin{array}{r} 7 \\ -1 \\ \hline \end{array}$
19. $\begin{array}{r} 8 \\ -6 \\ \hline \end{array}$
20. $\begin{array}{r} 7 \\ -3 \\ \hline \end{array}$

Problem Solving ▶ Number Sense

Write how many. Then circle the greater number.

21.

At Home Show 7 or 8 objects. Take some away. Ask your child to write a subtraction fact across and down to describe what you did.

Name_____

Act It Out With Models

There are **6** animals playing.
2 animals leave the game.
How many animals are still playing?

UNDERSTAND

What do you know?

- **6** animals are playing.
- **2** animals leave.

PLAN

Act it out.

Circle the model you would
use to act out the problem.

counters

cubes

SOLVE

Solve.

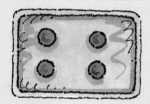

Show **6**.
Take away **2**.

There are _____ animals left.

LOOK BACK

How can you check your answer?

Remember to use the 4 steps.

Remember:
► Understand
► Plan
► Solve
► Look Back

Guided Practice

Act out the problem with counters.
Write the answer.

Draw or write to explain.

1. Kayla has 4 jars of jam. She gives 1 away. How many jars of jam does she have left?

Think
I start by showing 4 counters.

_____ jars of jam

2. Mike has 8 rabbits. 3 are brown. The other rabbits are white. How many rabbits are white?

Think
I know how many in all.
I know one part.

_____ white rabbits

Practice

3. There are 7 birds in the yard. 2 fly away. How many birds are left?

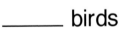

_____ birds

4. Tom has 5 apples. 2 apples are red. The rest are green. How many green apples does Tom have?

_____ green apples

Go on ►

Choose a Strategy

Solve.

1. Beth has **3** ears of corn. Ted has **3** ears of corn. How many ears of corn do they have in all?

Draw or write to explain.

ear of corn

_____ ears of corn

2. The farmer has **5** pumpkins. She gives **1** away. How many pumpkins does she have left?

pumpkin

_____ pumpkins

3. Damon plants **4** pumpkins. He plants **1** more watermelon than pumpkin. How many watermelons does Damon plant?

watermelon

_____ watermelons

4. **Multistep 3** rabbits are eating carrots. **2** more join them to eat. Then **1** rabbit leaves. How many rabbits are eating carrots now?

carrot

_____ rabbits

At Home Make up subtraction problems similar to those in the lesson. Ask your child to solve them.

Listening Skills

Listen to your teacher read the problem.
Solve.

1. Lucy has **6** peppers. She puts **2** in a salad. How many peppers does she have left?

Show your work using pictures, numbers, or words.

_____ peppers

2. There are **7** apples on a tree in the yard. **4** of the apples fall off. How many apples are still on the tree?

_____ apples

Listen to your teacher read the problem.
Choose the correct answer.

3. 2   3   4   8
       ○   ○   ○   ○

4. 2   3   4   6
       ○   ○   ○   ○

80 eighty

Write the difference.

1.

2.

$$4 - 4 = \underline{\hspace{2cm}}$$

$$5 - 0 = \underline{\hspace{2cm}}$$

Write the difference.

3. $8 - 3 = \underline{\hspace{1.5cm}}$ 4. $7 - 2 = \underline{\hspace{1.5cm}}$ 5. $7 - 3 = \underline{\hspace{1.5cm}}$

6. $8 - 1 = \underline{\hspace{1.5cm}}$ 7. $7 - 0 = \underline{\hspace{1.5cm}}$ 8. $8 - 6 = \underline{\hspace{1.5cm}}$

Write the difference.

9. $\begin{array}{r} 6 \\ -5 \\ \hline \end{array}$ 10. $\begin{array}{r} 8 \\ -4 \\ \hline \end{array}$ 11. $\begin{array}{r} 7 \\ -4 \\ \hline \end{array}$ 12. $\begin{array}{r} 8 \\ -7 \\ \hline \end{array}$ 13. $\begin{array}{r} 6 \\ -3 \\ \hline \end{array}$ 14. $\begin{array}{r} 7 \\ -1 \\ \hline \end{array}$

Choose a model and act out the problem.
Write the answer.

15. The baker has 7 pies.
    He sells 5 pies.
    How many pies are left?

Draw or write to explain.

_____ pies

Match. Circle the set with more.

1.

Match. Circle the set with fewer.

2.

```
<---+---+---+---+---+---+---+---+---+---+---+---+---+---+---+---+---+---+---+---+--->
    0   1   2   3   4   5   6   7   8   9  10  11  12  13  14  15  16  17  18  19  20
```

Circle the greater number.

3. 15   17   4. 9   8   5. 16   19

 Music
Connection

Musical Instruments

Some musical instruments are played with strings.

6 strings   4 strings   6 strings

guitar   violin   banjo

Which instrument has the fewest strings? _____

How many fewer strings does it have than the banjo? _____ strings

WEEKLY WR **READER** eduplace.com/kids/mw/

Vocabulary *e • Glossary*

Write a word to complete the sentence.

1. When you take away, you _____ .

2. The _____ tells how many are left.

| subtract |
| minus |
| difference |

Concepts and Skills

Listen to the story.
Draw counters to show the story.
Write the numbers.

3.

_____   _____ eaten   _____ left

Write how many yellow.

4.

Whole
4

Part	Part
1 ●	_____ ○

5.

Whole
5

Part	Part
4 ●	_____ ○

Circle and cross out to subtract.
Write how many are left.

6.

6 – 2 = _____

7.

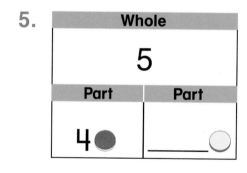

5 – 3 = _____

Write the difference.

8. $5 - 2 =$ _____

9. $6 - 5 =$ _____

10. $4 - 1 =$ _____

11.

$4 - 0 =$ _____

12.

$5 - 5 =$ _____

13. $8 - 3 =$ _____

14. $7 - 1 =$ _____

15. $8 - 2 =$ _____

16. $7 - 5 =$ _____

17. $8 - 4 =$ _____

18. $7 - 3 =$ _____

19.
$$\begin{array}{r} 6 \\ -3 \\ \hline \end{array}$$

20.
$$\begin{array}{r} 8 \\ -5 \\ \hline \end{array}$$

21.
$$\begin{array}{r} 7 \\ -6 \\ \hline \end{array}$$

22.
$$\begin{array}{r} 6 \\ -1 \\ \hline \end{array}$$

23.
$$\begin{array}{r} 8 \\ -7 \\ \hline \end{array}$$

24.
$$\begin{array}{r} 7 \\ -2 \\ \hline \end{array}$$

Problem Solving

Act out the problem with counters.

Write the answer.

25. There are 8 apples on a tree.
Mai picks 1 apple and eats it.
How many apples are left?

Draw or write to explain.

_____ apples

Data and Graphing

INVESTIGATION

Are there more children playing in the sandbox or with the ball?

People Using Math

Rachel Carson

Rachel Carson loved nature and science. She also liked to write. When she was ten years old, she had a story published.

Rachel became a marine biologist, someone who studies plants and animals in the sea. She wrote many books about caring for our planet.

Use tally marks to show how many people are in each family. Rachel lived with her mother, father, brother, and sister.

1.

Family Members	
Rachel's family	
My family	

Use the tally chart to make a pictograph.

2.

Family Members	
Rachel's family	
My family	

3. Does one family have more people? _____

4. **Write About It** What can you and your family do to help care for our planet? _____

_____

Name_____

Activity: Make a Tally Chart

Make 1 tally for each dot.

Objective
Represent data with tally marks.

Vocabulary
tally

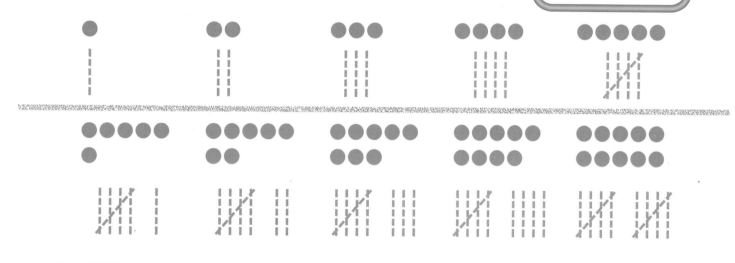

Work Together

Ask 10 friends which of these activities they like best.
Make 1 tally for each answer. Complete the tally chart.

1.

Activities

Think
Draw a line across for the fifth tally.

Use the tally chart.
Write how many children choose each activity.

2.  _____

3. _____

4.  _____

5. **Talk About It** How can you show 14 with tally marks?

1. Use the picture.
Complete the tally chart.

Cross out 1 child.
Then make 1 tally.

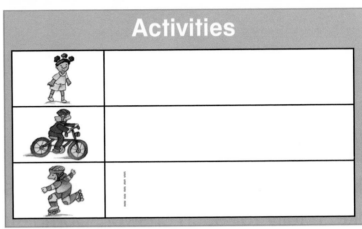

Activities

Use the tally chart to solve.

2. How many are there?

_____

3. How many are there?

_____

4. Which has the most? Circle.

5. Which has the fewest? Circle.

6. How many and are there?

_____ children

7. How many children are there in all?

_____ children

8. **Talk About It** Explain how you found the answer for Exercise 7.

At Home Pick three foods. Help your child survey family members or friends to find their favorite. Use tally marks to record the results.

Name_____

Read a Pictograph

MathTracks 1 / 11
Listen and Understand

A **pictograph** uses pictures to show information.
Each ⅄ stands for **1** child.

Children Playing

___4___ children are playing on the ![chicken].

Guided Practice

Children Playing

Use the pictograph to solve.
Each ⅄ stands for **1** child.

1. How many children played on the ![climber]?

   Think
   Count the ⅄ in the ![climber] row.

   _____ children

2. On which item do more children play? Circle.

3. On which item do the fewest children play? Circle.

TEST TIPS **Explain Your Thinking** How can you use the graph to tell if fewer children are on ![climber] or ![swing]?

What Children Drink

Use the pictograph to solve.
Each 🚶 stands for I child.

> Count the 🚶
> to find the answer.

1. How many children
   drink ?

   _5_ children

2. How many children drink
    and ?

   _____ children

3. Which do most children
   drink? Circle.

4. Which two drinks do the same
   number of children choose?
   Circle.

Algebra Readiness ▶ **Number Sentences**

Write a number sentence
to find the answer.

5. Mr. Lo has 8 .
   The children drink 3 🥛 .
   How many 🥛 are left?

   ___ ◯ ___ ◯ ___

   _____

At Home Use the pictograph above. Have your
child tell you what he or she knows about the graph.

Make a Pictograph

MathTracks 1 / 12
Listen and Understand

Objective
Make and use a pictograph to compare information.

You can make a pictograph.

Cross out one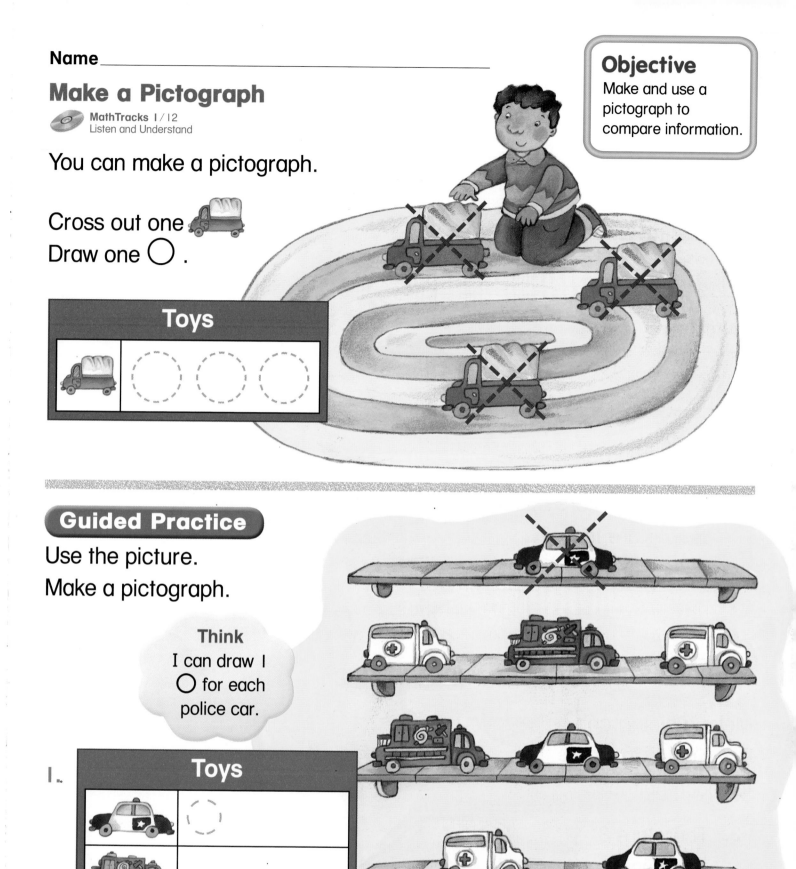
Draw one ○ .

Toys			
	◯	◯	◯

Guided Practice

Use the picture.
Make a pictograph.

Think
I can draw 1
○ for each
police car.

1.

Toys	
	◯

TEST TIPS **Explain Your Thinking** Which toy is shown the most?
Tell how you know.

Cross out 1 car, bus, or truck. Draw 1 wheel on the graph.

Use the picture.
Make a pictograph.

Driving on the Street

Use the pictograph to solve.

1. How many more  than ___ are there?

_____ more

2. How many ___ and ___ are there?

_____

Problem Solving ▶ Logical Thinking

Make a pictograph.
Draw a ⌒ to stand
for each helmet.

3. There are 3 .
There is 1 more
than .
There are 2 fewer
than .

Bike Helmets

4. **Talk About It** Which color has the most?
How do you know?

 At Home Help your child make a pictograph that tells about 3 food items in the house. Use store flyers to find pictures of food.

Go on ▶

Name_____

Writing Math: Create and Solve

You are taking a survey about the shoes your classmates are wearing. Write a question for your survey.

1. _____

_____

_____

Now, take the survey.
Make a pictograph.

2.

Write one thing you learned from the pictograph.

3. _____

_____

_____

Quick Check

Use the picture.
Complete the tally chart.

1.

Crayons	

Use the tally chart.
Complete the pictograph.

2.

Crayons	

3. How many more ▬▬▬ than ▬▬▬ are there?   _____ more

4. How many fewer ▬▬▬ than ▬▬▬ are there?   _____ fewer

5. How many ▬▬▬ and ▬▬▬ are there?   _____ in all

Name_____

Read a Bar Graph

MathTracks 1 / 13
Listen and Understand

Objective
Read a bar graph and use it to compare information.

Vocabulary
bar graph

This is a **bar graph.** It tells how many children choose each snack.

Snacks We Eat in School

Snacks

Number of Children

Guided Practice

Use the bar graph to solve.

1. How many children choose ?

   _____ children

   Think
   I look where the bar ends in the apple row.

2. How many children choose ?

   _____ children

3. Circle the snack more children choose.

4. Circle the snack fewer children choose.

TEST TIPS **Explain Your Thinking** If you choose a snack, how will the bar graph change?

Look at the number where the bar ends to know how many.

The bar graph shows the boats Nara sees.

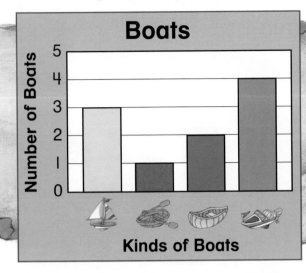

Use the bar graph to solve.

1. There are **4** of which kind of boat? Circle.

2. Are there fewer or ⬢ ? Circle.

3. How many ⛵ and 🛶 are there?

_____

4. How many more 🚤 than 🛶 are there?

_____ more

Reading Math ▶ Vocabulary

Show the tally marks for each number.

5. _____
   eleven

6. _____
   thirteen

7. _____
   eight

Choose a number. Make tally marks to show it.

8. ____ _____

At Home Ask your child questions about the graph above such as, how many more sailboats than rowboats are there?

Name_____

Activity: Make a Bar Graph

Work Together

Make a **tally chart.**
Ask **8** classmates their favorite color bike.
Make **1** tally for each answer.

Objective
Use a tally chart to make a bar graph and compare information.

Vocabulary
tally chart

1.

Favorite Bike Color	
🚲	
🚲	
🚲	
🚲	

Use the tally chart to make a bar graph.
Color **1** box for each tally.

Think
How many choose red?
I color that number of boxes.

2.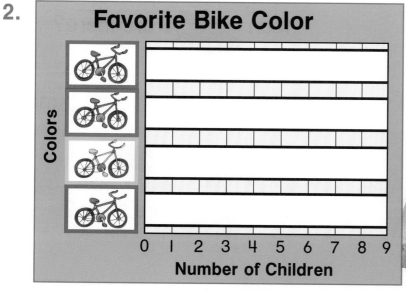

Favorite Bike Color

Colors

0 1 2 3 4 5 6 7 8 9
Number of Children

3. **Write About It** Make up a question about the bar graph.

_____

_____

On Your Own

I cross out 1 car.
Then I color 1 box.

Use the picture. Make a bar graph.

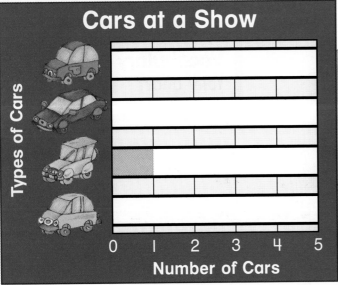

Cars at a Show

Types of Cars

Number of Cars
0 1 2 3 4 5

Use the bar graph to solve.

1. How many kinds of cars are there?

_____ kinds

2. How many are there?

_____

3. Circle the one that has 1 more than .

4. How many more 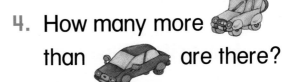 than are there?

_____ more

5. Are there fewer or ? Circle.

6. How many and are there?

_____

7. Circle which has the greatest number of cars.

8. Circle which has the least number of cars.

Go on

Name ____________________

Problem Solving ▶ Reasoning

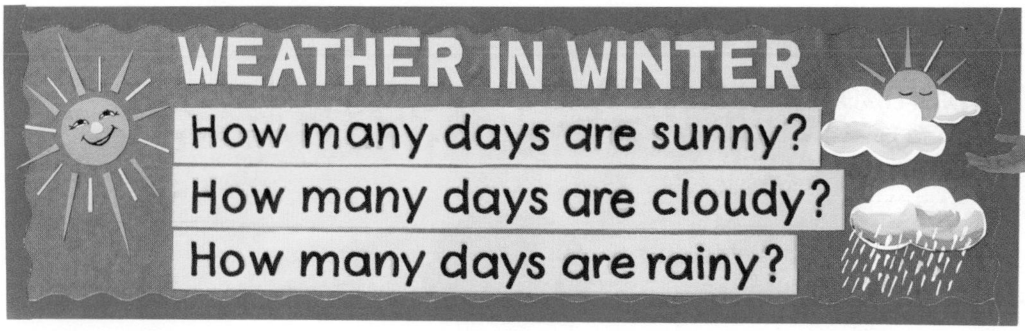
WEATHER IN WINTER
How many days are sunny?
How many days are cloudy?
How many days are rainy?

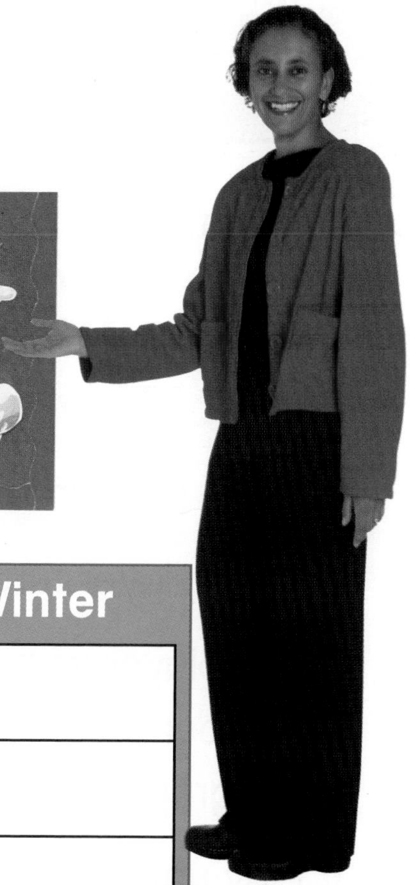

Ms. Bend's class is learning about weather. They made a chart to record the weather for 10 days.

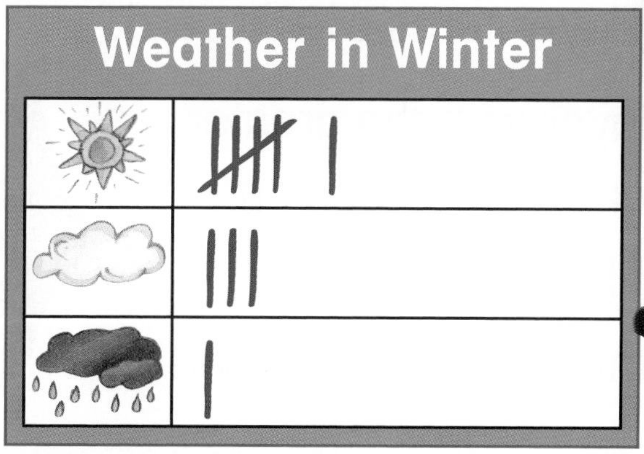
Weather in Winter

Use the tally chart to make a bar graph.
Label the graph.
Color the bars on the graph to show the weather.

1. 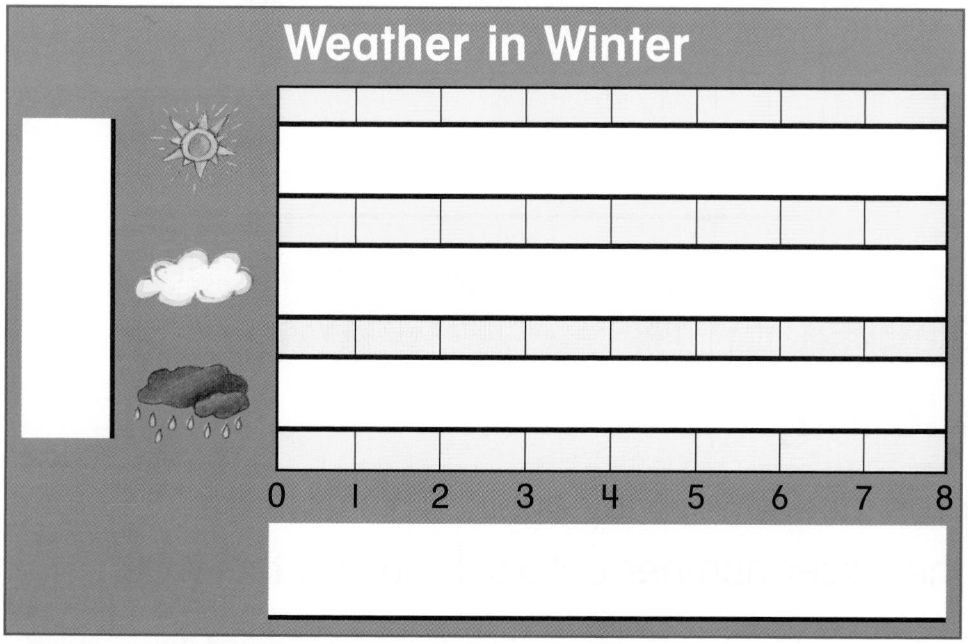
Weather in Winter
0
1
2
3
4
5
6
7
8

2. **Talk About It** What is the weather on most days? What else does the graph tell you?

At Home Ask your child to make a bar graph to show the number of windows in three rooms. Discuss the finished graph.

Numbers Are Great!

2 Players

What You Need: Number cards 1–20, blue crayon, red crayon

How to Play

1. Place the cards facedown in a pile.

2. Each player turns over a card.

3. The player with the greater number colors 1 box on the graph.

4. Play until all cards are used.

5. The player with the longer bar wins.

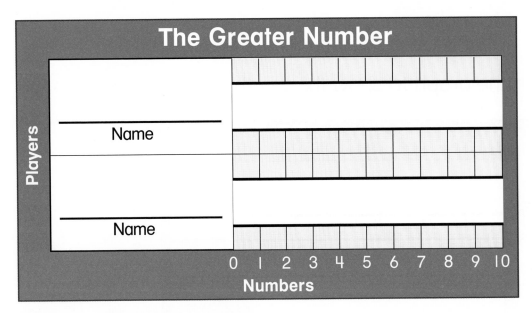

The Greater Number

Players — Name — Name

0 1 2 3 4 5 6 7 8 9 10

Numbers

Other Ways to Play

A. Place the cards facedown. Play again. This time the player with the lesser number colors 1 box on the graph.

B. Use a 0–5 spinner. Each player spins twice and adds the two numbers. The greater sum colors 1 box on the graph.

Name_____

Use a Graph

MathTracks 1 / 14
Listen and Understand

This graph shows how many boats are at one dock.

Objective
Use bar graphs to solve problems.

Boats at the Dock

Types of Boats

- Sailboat
- Motorboat
- Rowboat

0 1 2 3 4 5 6 7
Number of Boats

Use the graph, then add to solve the problem.

How many sailboats and rowboats in all?

Think
I can find the numbers on the graph. Then I add to find the sum.

3 sailboats
+ 4 rowboats
_____
7 in all

Use the graph, then subtract to solve the problem.

How many more motorboats are there than rowboats?

Think
I can find the numbers on the graph. Then I subtract to find the difference.

[ ] motorboats
− [ ] rowboats
_____
[ ] more motorboats

Chapter 4 Lesson 6

Use the bar graph to solve.

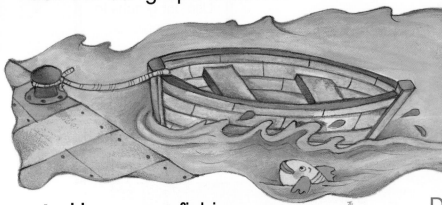

Boats at Pier 6

Types of Boats

Tanker

Fishing

Ferry

0 1 2 3 4 5 6 7
Number of Boats

1. How many fishing boats and ferry boats are there?

Think
I need to look at the bars next to Fishing and Ferry.

Draw or write to explain.

_____ boats

2. How many more tankers are there than ferry boats?

Think
I need to find how many more, so I subtract.

_____ more tankers

Practice

3. How many tankers and fishing boats are there?

_____ boats

4. How many more ferry boats are there than fishing boats?

_____ more ferry boat

Go on

Choose a Strategy

Solve.

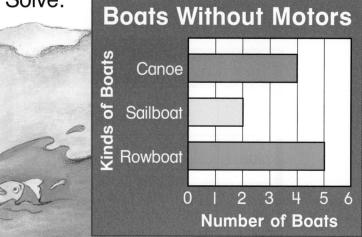

Boats Without Motors

Kinds of Boats

Canoe

Sailboat

Rowboat

0 1 2 3 4 5 6
Number of Boats

---

1. Use the bar graph. How many more rowboats are there than sailboats?

Draw or write to explain.

rowboat

_____ more rowboats

---

2. There are 4 canoes. One is red. The others are silver. How many are silver?

canoe

_____ silver

---

3. **Multistep** There are 5 people on a raft. 3 more people get on the raft. Then, 1 person jumps off the raft. How many people are on the raft now?

raft

_____ people

Chapter 4

At Home Ask questions that your child can answer by using the graph.

Problem-Solving for Tests

Listening Skills

Listen to your teacher read the problem.
Solve.

1. Frank's survey shows
   that 4 children like red.
   3 children like blue. 1 child
   likes yellow. Show what his
   pictograph looks like.

Favorite Colors	
red	
blue	
yellow	

2. Look at the pictograph.
   How many children
   answered the survey?

_____ children

Listen to your teacher read the problem.
Choose the correct answer.

Favorite Fruits	
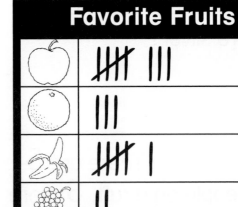 apple	IIII III
orange	III
banana	IIII I
grapes	II

3.

   ○   ○   ○   ○

4.   1   3   4   7

   ○   ○   ○   ○

1. Use the tally chart. Make the bar graph.

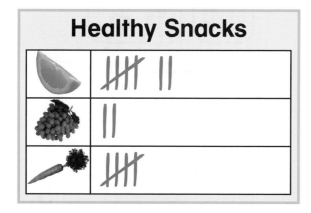

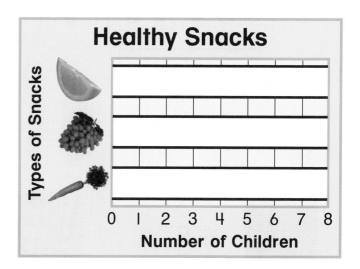

Use the bar graph to solve.

2. How many children like  the best?

_____ children

3. Circle the snack fewer children like.

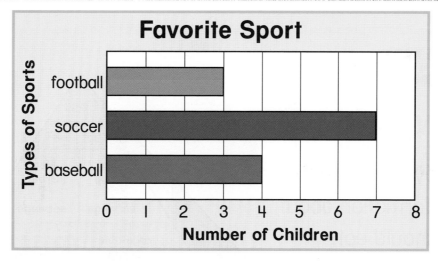

Use the bar graph to solve.

4. How many children choose football and baseball in all?

_____ children

5. How many more children choose soccer than football?

_____ more children

Write the sum.

1.

    5 + 1 = _____

2.

    2 + 3 = _____

3.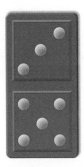

    $$\begin{array}{r} 3 \\ +5 \\ \hline \end{array}$$

4.

    $$\begin{array}{r} 6 \\ +0 \\ \hline \end{array}$$

5.

    $$\begin{array}{r} 5 \\ +2 \\ \hline \end{array}$$

Science Connection

Food Pyramid

The food pyramid is a way to show information about food you should eat.

- smaller parts stand for fewer servings of food

- larger parts stand for more servings of food

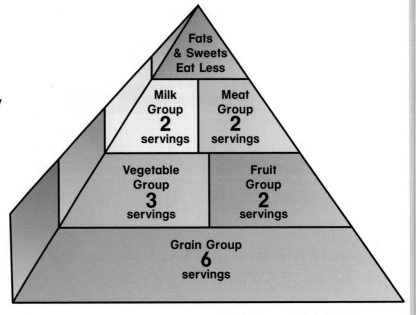

How many servings of vegetables should you eat? _____

Vocabulary  *e • Glossary*

Draw a line to match.

1. A **pictograph** uses

2. A **bar graph** uses

3. A **tally chart** uses

Concepts and Skills

4. Use the picture. Complete the tally chart.

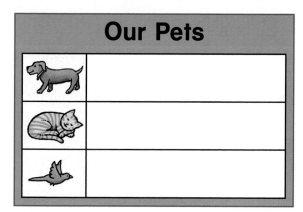

Our Pets

Use the tally chart to solve.

5. How many are there?

   _____

6. Which has the most? Circle.

---

7. Use the tally chart.
   Make the pictograph.

Our Pets

Use the pictograph to solve.

8. How many more than are there?

   _____ more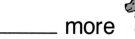

9. Which has the fewest? Circle.

10. Use the tally chart.
    Make a bar graph.

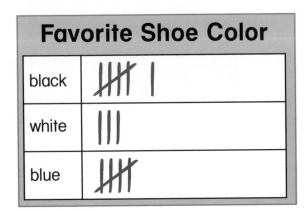

Favorite Shoe Color

black	IIII I
white	III
blue	IIII

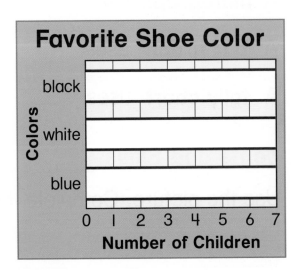

Favorite Shoe Color

11. How many children choose white shoes? _____ children

12. Do more children choose black or blue shoes?
    Circle.   black   blue

13. Circle the color fewer children choose.   black   white

Problem Solving

Use the bar graph to solve.

14. How many children like
    white and blue shoes?

    _____ children

15. How many more
    children like black
    shoes than blue shoes?

    _____ more

Name_____

America Recycles

It is important to recycle trash. Recycled trash can be used to make new things. Some towns have recycling centers where people can bring paper, glass, plastic, and metal.

Tallahassee, Florida celebrates America Recycles Day. There are contests and prizes. In one contest people estimate how many cans are in a recycling bin. People learn about recycling and have fun at the festival.

Complete the number sentence to solve.

1. Joe brings 3 glass bottles to the recycling center. Sachi brings 2 cans. How many items do they bring in all?

____ + ____ = ____

____ items

2. Jean collects 5 bags of newspapers for recycling. Elias collects 2 bags. How many bags do they collect altogether?

____ + ____ = ____

____ bags

3. Mrs. Baker has 7 plastic bottles. She takes 4 of them to the center. How many bottles are left?

____ − ____ = ____

____ bottles

Recycling helps take care of the trash problem. It also helps our Earth in other ways.

- Recycling paper can save trees.
- Glass can be recycled over and over.
- More than 1 thousand cans are recycled in 1 second in America.

Used Item ⟶ Recycled Item

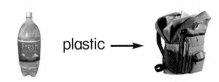
paper ⟶

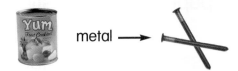
plastic ⟶

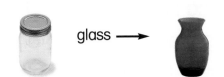
metal ⟶

glass ⟶

People Recycling

Use the pictograph to solve.

1. How many people recycle ?

_____ people

2. Which item do people recycle the most? Circle.

3. How many people recycle and ?

_____ people

4. How many people recycle and ?

_____ people

Technology
Visit *Education Place* at **eduplace.com/kids/mw/** to learn more about this topic.

 **Unit I Test**

Vocabulary  *e* • Glossary

| addend |
| difference |

Write the word to complete the sentence.

1. An _____ is a number added in an addition problem.

2. The _____ is the answer to a subtraction problem.

Concepts and Skills

Count. Write the number.

3.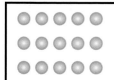

_____
seven

4.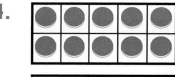

_____
twenty

5.

_____
four

6.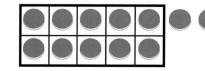

_____
thirteen

Circle the words that make the sentence true.

7.

15   is greater than   12
        is less than

8.

9   is equal to   9
        is less than

9.

4   is greater than   7
        is less than

10.

18   is greater than   16
        is less than

Write the sum.

11. 4
   +4
   ___

12. 1
   +6
   ___

13. 0
   +3
   ___

Write the difference.

14. 3
   −3
   ___

15. 8
   −7
   ___

16. 7
   −5
   ___

Use the picture.
Make a pictograph.

17.

Toys	

18. How many  are there?

   _____

19. How many more  than _____ are there?

   _____ more

Problem Solving

Write an addition sentence to solve.
Write the answer.

20. There are 5 ants on the hill.
    3 more ants join them.
    How many ants in all?

   _____ ants

Complete the pictograph.
Draw a 🧍 for each child.

1. **2** children like 🍎 best.
   5 children like 🍌 best.
   3 children like 🍇 best.

Fruits We Like

🍎	
🍌	
🍇	

Complete the bar graph.

2. **2** children like green.
   6 children like blue.
   4 children like red.

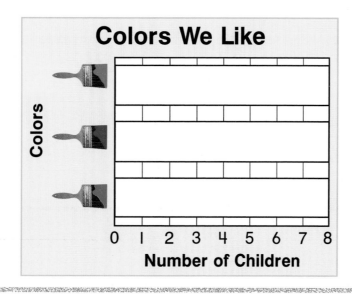

Colors We Like

Colors

0 1 2 3 4 5 6 7 8
Number of Children

Solve.

3. There are **4** red flowers in a pot.
   Taro plants **3** blue flowers in the pot.
   How many flowers in all?

Show your work using pictures, numbers, or words.

_____ flowers

Estimation

Estimate how many.

1. Circle the group that has more left.

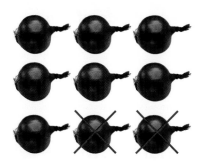

2. Circle the group that has more than **5** left.

Estimate.
Count to check your answer.

3. Chan estimates there are about **50** strawberries. Teva says there are about **200** strawberries. Who is right?

_____

4. Count **10** books on the library shelf. Now estimate how many books in all.

10 books

_____ books

 Technology

Visit *Education Place* at **eduplace.com/kids/mw/** for brain teasers.

Calculator
Use a Bar Graph

A can help you compare numbers on a bar graph.

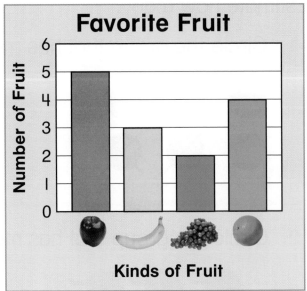

Favorite Fruit

Number of Fruit

Kinds of Fruit

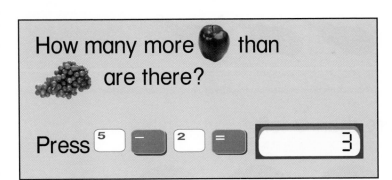

How many more 🍎 than 🍇 are there?

Press ⁵ − ² = | 3

Use and the bar graph.

1. How many and 🍊 are there?

_____ in all

2. How many fewer than are there?

_____ fewer

3. How many 🍇 and 🍊 are there in all?

_____ in all

4. Circle the one that has 2 fewer fruit than .

Explain Your Thinking How many pieces of fruit are there altogether?

Test-Taking Tips

• •

Read each question two times.

Fill in the correct ○ .

If you are not sure how to find the
answer, go on to the next question.

Multiple Choice

Fill in the ○ for the correct answer.

1. Count the ●.
   Choose the number.

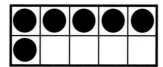

4	5	6	7
○	○	○	○

3. Add. How many in all?

2	3	4	5
○	○	○	○

2. Add. Find the sum.

$$4 + 0 = \underline{}$$

0	2	3	4
○	○	○	○

4. Subtract. How many
   are left?

3	5	7	8
○	○	○	○

Fill in the ○ for the correct answer.
NH means Not Here.

5. Subtract. Find the difference.

$$\begin{array}{r} 7 \\ -5 \\ \hline \end{array}$$

2	3	4	NH
○	○	○	○

6. How many children have  ?

Our Pets

1	3	5	7
○	○	○	○

7. How many sunny days does the graph show?

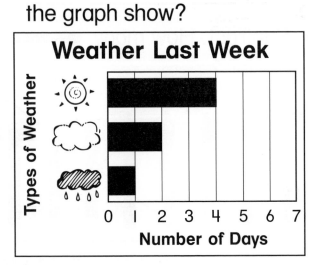

1	2	3	4
○	○	○	○

Solve.

8. There are 5 bees on the flower. 2 more bees join them. How many bees in all?

_____ bees

9. Alita has 6 balloons. 3 balloons pop. How many are left?

_____ balloons

10. Look at the picture. Write an addition sentence.

_____

Test Prep on the Net
Visit *Education Place* at
eduplace.com/kids/mw/
for more test prep practice.

118 one hundred eighteen

Addition and Subtraction Facts Through 10

From the Read-Aloud Anthology

Bug Fun!

by Sarah Curran

illustrated by Mike Gibbie

Access Prior Knowledge

This story will help you review

- Counting
- Number sentences

3 little ants soon strike out.
The others give a great big shout.
Now 4 ants wait to hit the ball.
How many ants are there in all?

3 + 4 = _____ ants

All the grasshoppers take a dip.
They are careful not to slip.
Then **2** grasshoppers hop away.
How many grasshoppers stay to play?

6 − 2 = _____ grasshoppers

Name _____

Use the pictures on pages 119a, 119b, and 119c.

1. How many bugs are on page 119a?   _____ bugs

2. On page 119b there are ants wearing red or
   purple shirts.

   How many ants are wearing red shirts?   _____ ants

   How many ants are wearing purple shirts?   _____ ants

   How many ants are there in all?

   _____ + _____ = _____   _____ ants

3. On page 119c there are 4 grasshoppers playing
   and 2 running away. How many grasshoppers
   will be left playing if 2 more leave?

   $4 - 2 =$ _____   _____ grasshoppers

4. Look at the pictures on pages 119b and 119c.
   How many ants in red and grasshoppers in
   the water are there?

   _____ + _____ = _____   _____ bugs

120

Dear Family,

My class is starting Unit 2. I will be learning about strategies to help me with addition and subtraction facts through 10. These pages show what I will learn and have activities for us to do together.

From, _____

Vocabulary

These are some words I will use in this unit.

count on A strategy used to add

Find 5 + 2.
Say 5.
Count 6, 7.
5 + 2 = 7

count back A strategy used to subtract

Find 8 − 3.
Say 8.
Count 7, 6, 5.
8 − 3 = 5

number line A diagram that shows numbers in order as equally spaced points on a line

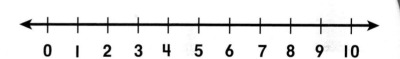

Some other words I may use are **addend** and **double**.

Vocabulary Activity

Let's work together to complete these sentences.

1. I can _____ to find 6 − 3.

2. I can _____ to find 8 + 2.

Turn the page for more.

How To use strategies to add and subtract

These counting on and counting back problems are examples of what I will be learning.

Counting on

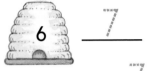 6 | _7_

6 + 1 = _7_

  6 | _7_ , _8_

6 + 2 = _8_

Counting back

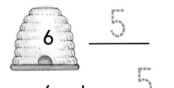 6 | _5_

6 − 1 = _5_

  6 | _5_ , _4_

6 − 2 = _4_

◆ Literature

These books link to the math in this unit. We can look for them at the library.

Addition Annie
by David Gisler
Illustrated by Sarah A. Beise
(Children's Press, 2002)

The Right Number of Elephants
by Jeff Sheppard

Two of Everything
by Lily Toy Hong

Let's read together!

Technology

We can visit *Education Place* at **eduplace.com/parents/mw/** for the Math Lingo game, *e* • Glossary, and more games and activities to do together.

Addition Strategies Through 10

CHAPTER 5

INVESTIGATION

How many ants and bees are there altogether?

Flower Fun

Listen to your teacher.

Name_____

Count On to Add

You can **count on** to add.

Find 7 + 2.
Start with 7. Count on 2.

7   _8_ , _9_

7 + 2 = _9_

Find 7 + 3.
Start with 7. Count on 3.

7   _8_ , _9_ , _10_

7 + 3 = _10_

Guided Practice

Count on to add.

Think
I start with 7.
I count on 1.

1.

7   ____

7 + 1 = ___

2.

8   ____ , ____

8 + 2 = ___

3.

 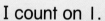

6   ____ , ____ , ____

6 + 3 = ____

4.

9   ____

9 + 1 = ____

TEST TIPS **Explain Your Thinking** Count on to find 9 + 3.
Do you count on the same way to find 3 + 9? Why?

Count on 1, 2, or 3.

Count on to add.

1.

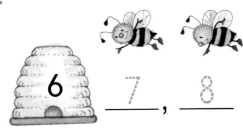

6

___7___ , ___8___

6 + 2 = ___8___

2.

6

_____

6 + 1 = ___

---

3. 5 + 1 = ___   4. 8 + 1 = ___   5. 4 + 2 = ___

6. 5 + 2 = ___   7. 6 + 3 = ___   8. 9 + 1 = ___

---

9. 6
   +2

10. 7
   +3

11. 3
   +1

12. 8
   +2

13. 4
   +1

14. 5
   +3

15. 3
   +2

16. 8
   +1

17. 2
   +1

18. 7
   +2

19. 9
   +1

20. 4
   +3

21. 7
   +1

22. 5
   +2

23. 6
   +1

24. 3
   +2

25. 5
   +1

26. 6
   +3

Problem Solving ▶ Visual Thinking

27. How many and ?

[ ]

At Home Say a number from 1 through 8. Have your child count on 2 and then say the addition fact.

Name_____

Use a Number Line to Add

Find the greater number on the **number line.**
Count on.

Objective
Find sums through 10 by counting on a number line.

Vocabulary
number line

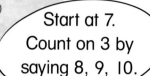

Start at 7.
Count on 3 by
saying 8, 9, 10.

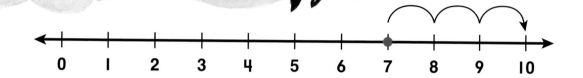

3 + 7 = __10__

Guided Practice

Use the number line.
Find the sum.

Think
6 is the greater
number. Say 6.
Count 7, 8, 9.

1. 6 + 3 = _____

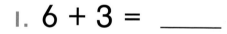

2. 5 + 2 = _____

3. 2 + 7 = _____

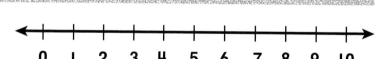

4. 9
   +1
   ___

5. 1
   +8
   ___

6. 8
   +2
   ___

7. 6
   +2
   ___

8. 3
   +6
   ___

9. 7
   +1
   ___

TEST TIPS **Explain Your Thinking** Why is it helpful to start with
the greater number?

Start with the greater number.

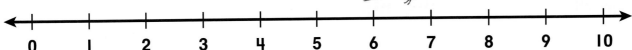

```
  0   1   2   3   4   5   6   7   8   9   10
```

Use the number line.
Find the sum.

1. $4 + 2 =$ __6__

2. $1 + 7 =$ ____

3. $8 + 2 =$ ____

4. $3 + 5 =$ ____

5. $1 + 6 =$ ____

6. $2 + 3 =$ ____

7. $2 + 4 =$ ____

8. $3 + 1 =$ ____

9. $1 + 9 =$ ____

10.
$$\begin{array}{r} 2 \\ +1 \\ \hline \end{array}$$

11.
$$\begin{array}{r} 3 \\ +4 \\ \hline \end{array}$$

12.
$$\begin{array}{r} 7 \\ +3 \\ \hline \end{array}$$

13.
$$\begin{array}{r} 1 \\ +5 \\ \hline \end{array}$$

14.
$$\begin{array}{r} 5 \\ +2 \\ \hline \end{array}$$

15.
$$\begin{array}{r} 2 \\ +6 \\ \hline \end{array}$$

16.
$$\begin{array}{r} 9 \\ +1 \\ \hline \end{array}$$

17.
$$\begin{array}{r} 2 \\ +5 \\ \hline \end{array}$$

18.
$$\begin{array}{r} 1 \\ +4 \\ \hline \end{array}$$

19.
$$\begin{array}{r} 3 \\ +2 \\ \hline \end{array}$$

20.
$$\begin{array}{r} 2 \\ +8 \\ \hline \end{array}$$

21.
$$\begin{array}{r} 3 \\ +7 \\ \hline \end{array}$$

Problem Solving ▶ Number Sense

Use the number line.

22. What number is 2 more than 8? ____

23. What number is 3 more than 7? ____

24. What number is 2 more than 5? ____

 **At Home** Have your child use the number line to add 1, 2, or 3 to any number less than 8.

Use Doubles to Add

 MathTracks 1 / 15
Listen and Understand

A **double** fact has two **addends** that are the same.

Objective
Add using doubles and doubles plus one.

Vocabulary
double   addend

This is a double.

This is a double plus one.

 4 + 4 and 1 more.

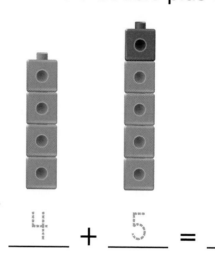

__4__ + __4__ = __8__
addend   addend   sum

__4__ + __5__ = __9__

Guided Practice

Complete the addition sentence.

1.

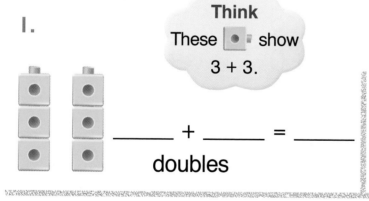

Think
These ▣ show 3 + 3.

_____ + _____ = _____
doubles

_____ + _____ = _____
doubles plus one

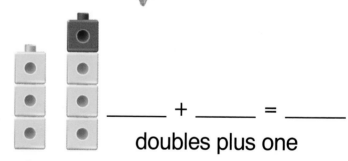

2.

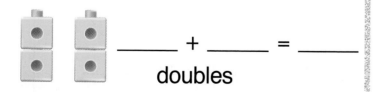

_____ + _____ = _____
doubles

_____ + _____ = _____
doubles plus one

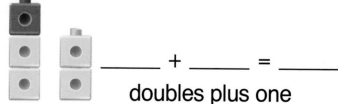

TEST TIPS **Explain Your Thinking** How does knowing $2 + 2 = 4$ help you find $3 + 2$?

Practice

Use doubles to help you find the sum.

Write the sum.

1. 3 + 3 = __6__   3 + 4 = __7__   4 + 3 = __7__

2. 4 + 4 = ____   4 + 5 = ____   5 + 4 = ____

3. 2   2   3
   +2   +3   +2
   ___   ___   ___

4. 1   1   2
   +1   +2   +1
   ___   ___   ___

5. 4   6. 3   7. 4   8. 4   9. 3   10. 5
   +5   +3   +4   +3   +4   +5
   ___   ___   ___   ___   ___   ___

11. 0   12. 1   13. 5   14. 2   15. 7   16. 5
    +8   +5   +3   +4   +2   +4
    ___   ___   ___   ___   ___   ___

17. 3   18. 2   19. 2   20. 9   21. 3   22. 4
    +7   +8   +6   +0   +6   +3
    ___   ___   ___   ___   ___   ___

Algebra Readiness ▶ Missing Addends

Choose a number to make a double.

23.   4   24. ☐   25. ☐   26.   1
    + ☐   + 3   + 5   + ☐
    ____   ____   ____   ____
      8   6   10   2

At Home Say a doubles plus one fact such as 3 + 4.
Ask your child to name the double that helps find the sum.

Go on ➡

Name_____

Doubles or Not

2 Players

What You Need: 2 number cubes (0–5 on each),
2 two-color counters

How to Play

Take turns.

1. Roll the cubes.
2. Find the sum.
3. Use the table to find how to move your ◯.

Roll	Move
doubles plus one	3 spaces
doubles	2 spaces
any other fact	1 space

Continue to play until a player reaches the end.

START

Ahead 1 space

Roll again

Back 1 space

Back 1 space

END

Lose turn

Roll again

Quick Check

Count on to add.

1. $7 + 3 =$ _____   2. $9 + 1 =$ _____   3. $6 + 2 =$ _____

Find the sum.

4. $\begin{array}{r} 1 \\ +5 \\ \hline \end{array}$ 5. $\begin{array}{r} 2 \\ +7 \\ \hline \end{array}$

```
←——+——+——+——+——+——+——+——+——+——+——→
   0   1   2   3   4   5   6   7   8   9   10
```

6. $\begin{array}{r} 4 \\ +4 \\ \hline \end{array}$ 7. $\begin{array}{r} 5 \\ +4 \\ \hline \end{array}$ 8. $\begin{array}{r} 3 \\ +3 \\ \hline \end{array}$ 9. $\begin{array}{r} 4 \\ +3 \\ \hline \end{array}$ 10. $\begin{array}{r} 4 \\ +5 \\ \hline \end{array}$

Math Challenge

Doubles Rule

Use the rule.
Complete the table.

Add the double.	
1	2
2	
3	
4	

Add the double plus one.	
1	3
2	
3	
4	

Using Addition Strategies

MathTracks 1/16
Listen and Understand

Ways to Add

Count on
Use a number line
Use doubles
Use counters
Draw a picture

There are different ways to find a sum.

Guided Practice

Choose a way to add.
Write the sum.

1. 4
   +5

Think
4 + 4 is a double fact. 4 + 5 is one more.

2. 9
   +1

3. 6
   +1

4. 5
   +5

5. 3
   +4

6. 6
   +4

7. 1
   +8

8. 4
   +2

9. 7
   +3

10. 5
   +0

11. 3 + 0 = _____

12. 4 + 6 = _____

13. 3 + 5 = _____

14. 1 + 2 = _____

15. 6 + 3 = _____

16. 3 + 2 = _____

TEST TIPS **Explain Your Thinking** How did you add 3 + 2? Why?

Choose a way to add.

Ways to Add
Count on
Use a number line
Use doubles
Use counters
Draw a picture

Write the sum.

1. 1
    +5
    ___
    6

2. 5
    +3
    ___

3. 6
    +0
    ___

4. 2
    +5
    ___

5. 6
    +3
    ___

6. 0
    +9
    ___

7. 8
    +2
    ___

8. 2
    +4
    ___

9. 0
    +10
    ___

10. 5
    +5
    ___

11. 2
    +6
    ___

12. 2
    +2
    ___

13. 6
    +2
    ___

14. 4
    +6
    ___

15. 3
    +4
    ___

16. 4
    +3
    ___

17. 1 + 1 = ____

18. 6 + 4 = ____

19. 5 + 1 = ____

20. 5 + 4 = ____

21. 2 + 8 = ____

22. 3 + 6 = ____

Problem Solving ▶ Logical Thinking

Use the clues. Find each snail.
Write the correct letter.

23. Snail A has

Snail B has

Snail C has

Snail D has

____ ____ ____ ____

At Home Ask your child to tell one way to solve 6 + 3.

Name_____

Write a Number Sentence

Erin looks for ants.
She finds a group of **3** red ants
and a group of **4** black ants.
How many ants does Erin find in all?

Objective
Use parts and wholes
and number sentences
to solve problems.

UNDERSTAND

What do you know?

- Erin finds **3** red ants.
- Erin finds **4** black ants.

Whole	
Red	Black
🐜 🐜 🐜	🐜 🐜 🐜 🐜

PLAN

You know the parts.
You need to find the whole.
Circle how you would solve the
problem.

add

subtract

SOLVE

Write a number sentence.

__3__ ⊕ __4__ ◯ __7__

Erin finds __7__ ants in all.

Whole	
7	
Part	Part
3	4

LOOK BACK

How do you know your answer makes sense?

Guided Practice

Remember to use
the 4 steps.

Remember:
▶ Understand
▶ Plan
▶ Solve
▶ Look Back

Use Workmat 3 and ◯ .

Write a number sentence to solve.

1. Marta sees 4 beetles.
   Brian sees 6 beetles.
   How many beetles do
   both children see?

   Think
   I add to find
   how many.

   ___ ◯ ___ ◯ ___

   _____ beetles

2. There are 6 moths near
   the light. 3 more
   moths fly to the light.
   How many moths are
   near the light now?

   Think
   One part is 6.
   The other part
   is 3.

   ___ ◯ ___ ◯ ___

   _____ moths

Practice

3. There are 4 fireflies in the
   air. 4 fireflies are in the
   grass. How many fireflies
   are there altogether?

   ___ ◯ ___ ◯ ___

   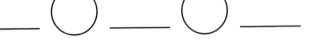

   _____ fireflies

4. There is 1 flea on the dog.
   Then, 2 more fleas land on
   the dog. How many fleas
   are on the dog now?

   ___ ◯ ___ ◯ ___

   _____ fleas

Go on ➡

Name_____

Strategies
Draw a Picture
Write a Number Sentence
Act It Out With Models

Choose a Strategy

Solve.

1. There are 5 ladybugs on a leaf. 2 more ladybugs join them. How many ladybugs are on the leaf now?

Draw or write to explain.

ladybug

_____ ladybugs

2. Mr. Ray sees 1 caterpillar on a log. Hailey sees 4 caterpillars on a log. How many caterpillars do they see on the log?

caterpillar

_____ caterpillars

3. Sofia counts 3 butterflies on a bush and 2 butterflies flying nearby. How many butterflies does she count in all?

butterfly

_____ butterflies

4. **Multistep** David sees 6 dragonflies over the creek and 2 by the reeds. Then he sees 1 more by the sand. How many dragonflies does he see?

dragonfly

_____ dragonflies

At Home Use groups of 10 or fewer objects around you. Create addition problems that your child can solve.

Listen to your teacher read the problem.
Solve.

1. The class sees 6 bees on the hive. They see 2 bees on a flower. How many bees do they see altogether?

Show your work using pictures, numbers, or words.

_____ bees

2. There are 2 crickets in the grass. 5 crickets are on the path. How many crickets are there?

_____ crickets

Listen to your teacher read the problem.
Choose the correct answer.

3.   1   5   6   10
     ○   ○   ○   ○

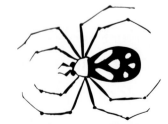

4.   5   8   9   10
     ○   ○   ○   ○

Quick Check

Write the sum.

1. $8 + 2 =$ _____   2. $1 + 4 =$ _____   3. $6 + 3 =$ _____

4. $\begin{array}{r} 1 \\ +9 \\ \hline \end{array}$ 5. $\begin{array}{r} 5 \\ +2 \\ \hline \end{array}$ 6. $\begin{array}{r} 7 \\ +2 \\ \hline \end{array}$ 7. $\begin{array}{r} 3 \\ +5 \\ \hline \end{array}$ 8. $\begin{array}{r} 2 \\ +4 \\ \hline \end{array}$

9. $0 + 6 =$ _____   10. $4 + 5 =$ _____   11. $3 + 6 =$ _____

12. $3 + 4 =$ _____   13. $4 + 4 =$ _____   14. $3 + 0 =$ _____

15. $\begin{array}{r} 5 \\ +5 \\ \hline \end{array}$ 16. $\begin{array}{r} 9 \\ +0 \\ \hline \end{array}$ 17. $\begin{array}{r} 5 \\ +3 \\ \hline \end{array}$ 18. $\begin{array}{r} 4 \\ +6 \\ \hline \end{array}$ 19. $\begin{array}{r} 7 \\ +3 \\ \hline \end{array}$

Write a number sentence to solve.

20. Jessie finds 6 small rocks and 1 large rock. How many rocks does he find in all?

_____ $\bigcirc$ _____ $\bigcirc$ _____

_____ rocks

Use the picture. Complete the tally chart.

1.

Insects	

Use the tally chart to solve.

2. How many ?

_____

3. How many ?

_____

4. Which has more?

5. Which has fewer?

Science Connection

Caterpillar to Butterfly

A caterpillar hatches from an egg. In 4 weeks it wraps itself in a chrysalis. In 3 weeks the chrysalis opens. Out comes a butterfly.

About how many weeks does it take to change from caterpillar to butterfly?

_____

Vocabulary ⓔ Glossary

1. Circle the **addends** in this fact.

   5 + 4 = 9

2. How do you use a **number line**?
   Circle.

   to count on   to add doubles

3. Write a **double** fact.

   _____

Concepts and Skills

Count on to add.

4. 9 + 1 = ____   5. 5 + 2 = ____   6. 6 + 2 = ____

Find the sum.

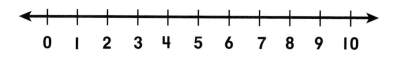

0   1   2   3   4   5   6   7   8   9   10

7. 8 + 1 = ____   8. 1 + 9 = ____   9. 2 + 4 = ____

Write the sum.

10.	11.	12.	13.	14.	15.
4 +4	4 +5	5 +4	3 +3	4 +3	3 +4

16.	17.	18.	19.	20.	21.
0 +9	6 +4	7 +3	5 +4	8 +2	3 +6

Problem Solving

Write a number sentence to solve.

22. Gia sees **7** bumble bees and **1** honey bee. How many bees does she see in all?

_____ bees

23. There are **5** red ants and **4** black ants. How many ants are there altogether?

_____ ants

24. Jon finds **1** beetle. Then he finds **5** more. How many beetles does Jon find?

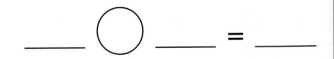

_____ beetles

25. There are **3** ladybugs on one leaf. There are **2** ladybugs on another. How many ladybugs are there in all?

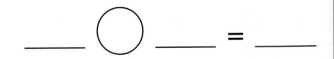

_____ ladybugs

Subtraction Strategies Through 10

CHAPTER 6

INVESTIGATION

When this girl takes her lamb away, how many lambs will be left?

People Using Math
· · · · · · · · · · · · · · · · · · · ·

James Herriot

James Herriot was a man who loved animals. He became a veterinarian, a doctor that takes care of animals. He took care of farm animals and pets. Dogs were his favorite animals, and he had many dogs during his life.

James Herriot, author of
All Creatures Great and Small

Use the picture to solve the problems.

1. How many dogs are there? _____ dogs

2. How many ears are there altogether? _____ ears

   If one dog walks away, how many ears are left?

   ____ ◯ ____ ◯ ____   _____ ears

3. How many tails are there altogether? _____ tails

   If one dog walks away, how many tails are left?

   ____ ◯ ____ ◯ ____   _____ tails

4. **Talk About It** If you could choose any animal for a pet, what would you choose?

Name_____

Count Back to Subtract

You can **count back** to subtract.

Start with 9. Count back 2.

9   ___8___ , ___7___

9 − 2 = ___7___

Start with 9. Count back 3.

9   ___8___ , ___7___ , ___6___

9 − 3 = ___6___

Guided Practice

Count back to subtract.

Think
I start with 10.
I count back 2.

1.

10   _____ , _____

10 − 2 = _____

2.

10   _____ , _____ , _____

10 − 3 = _____

3.

10   _____

10 − 1 = _____

4.

9   _____

9 − 1 = _____

TEST TIPS **Explain Your Thinking** How do you count back to find 8 − 2?

Count back 1, 2, or 3.

Count back to subtract.

1.

8

7, 6, 5

8 − 3 = 5

2.

8

_____, _____

8 − 2 = ____

3. 10 − 3 = ____   4. 10 − 2 = ____   5. 10 − 1 = ____

6. 7 − 2 = ____   7. 9 − 1 = ____   8. 2 − 2 = ____

9. 6
   −3

10. 10
    − 1

11. 7
    −1

12. 6
    −2

13. 5
    −1

14. 7
    −2

15. 9
    −3

16. 10
    − 2

17. 8
    −3

18. 9
    −2

19. 8
    −2

20. 7
    −3

Problem Solving ▶ Reasoning

21. There are 4 sheep.
    2 of the sheep are black.
    How many sheep are white?

Draw or write to explain.

_____ white sheep

At Home Say a number from 4 through 10. Have your child use
counting back to subtract 1, 2, or 3.

Use a Number Line to Subtract

Use a **number line** to find $10 - 3$.

Objective
Subtract using a number line.

Vocabulary
number line

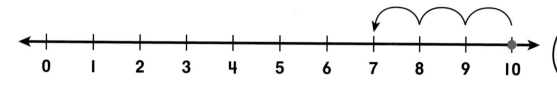

$10 - 3 = \underline{7}$

Start at 10.
Count back 3 by
saying 9, 8, 7.

Think
9 is the greater number.
Say 9. Count 8, 7.

Guided Practice

Write the difference.

1. $9 - 2 = \underline{}$

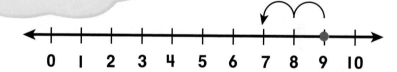

2. $10 - 1 = \underline{}$

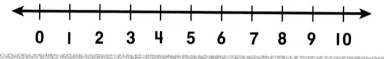

3. $8 - 3 = \underline{}$

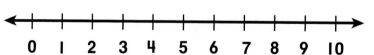

4. $\begin{array}{r} 10 \\ -\ 2 \\ \hline \end{array}$
5. $\begin{array}{r} 9 \\ -3 \\ \hline \end{array}$
6. $\begin{array}{r} 7 \\ -1 \\ \hline \end{array}$
7. $\begin{array}{r} 6 \\ -3 \\ \hline \end{array}$
8. $\begin{array}{r} 5 \\ -1 \\ \hline \end{array}$
9. $\begin{array}{r} 8 \\ -2 \\ \hline \end{array}$

TEST TIPS **Explain Your Thinking** Tell how you can
use the number line to find $8 - 3$.

Find the number you are subtracting from on the number line.

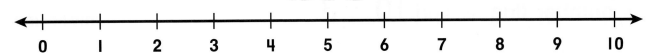

0   1   2   3   4   5   6   7   8   9   10

Write the difference.

1. $9 - 1 =$ ___8___

2. $10 - 2 =$ ____

3. $7 - 1 =$ ____

4. $6 - 3 =$ ____

5. $6 - 1 =$ ____

6. $7 - 2 =$ ____

7. $\begin{array}{r} 6 \\ -2 \\ \hline \end{array}$

8. $\begin{array}{r} 10 \\ -\ 3 \\ \hline \end{array}$

9. $\begin{array}{r} 8 \\ -1 \\ \hline \end{array}$

10. $\begin{array}{r} 7 \\ -3 \\ \hline \end{array}$

11. $\begin{array}{r} 5 \\ -3 \\ \hline \end{array}$

12. $\begin{array}{r} 6 \\ -3 \\ \hline \end{array}$

13. $\begin{array}{r} 9 \\ -2 \\ \hline \end{array}$

14. $\begin{array}{r} 10 \\ -\ 1 \\ \hline \end{array}$

15. $\begin{array}{r} 3 \\ -1 \\ \hline \end{array}$

16. $\begin{array}{r} 8 \\ -3 \\ \hline \end{array}$

17. $\begin{array}{r} 7 \\ -2 \\ \hline \end{array}$

18. $\begin{array}{r} 5 \\ -1 \\ \hline \end{array}$

Problem Solving ▶ Reasoning

19. Molly sees 10 pigs.
3 pigs walk away.
How many pigs are left?

Draw or write to explain.

_____ pigs

20. The 3 pigs come back.
How many pigs does
Molly see now?

_____ pigs

At Home Help your child make a number line. Ask him or her to show you how to use it to subtract.

How Many More? How Many Fewer?

 MathTracks 1/17
Listen and Understand

How many more than are there?

Match the to the .

Count how many more than .

You can subtract to compare sets of objects.

$8 - 3 = \underline{5}$

There are 5 more 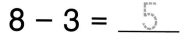 than .

Guided Practice

Match. Then subtract.

1. How many fewer than are there?

Think
Match 4
to 4 .
How many do not
have a match?

$9 - 4 = \underline{}$

TEST TIPS **Explain Your Thinking** Can you add to compare sets of objects? Why?

Objective
Show the meaning of subtraction by comparing.

Count how many do not have a match.

Match. Then subtract.

1. How many more than are there?

$8 - 6 = \underline{2}$

2. How many fewer than ?

$9 - 5 = \underline{}$

3. How many more than are there?

$10 - 4 = \underline{}$

Problem Solving ▶ Reasoning

4. Ratta sees **6** cows.
   Then she sees **4** more.
   How many cows does
   Ratta see?

Draw or write to explain.

_____ cows

At Home Make two sets of objects; one with 10 and one with less than 10. Have your child subtract to compare the sets.

Go on ▶

Writing Math: Create and Solve

Write a subtraction story that compares the birds.

1. _____

_____

_____

Write the subtraction sentence.

2. ____ ◯ ____ ◯ ____

Tell a story to match the number sentence.   7 – 4 = 3

Draw a picture to show your story.

3.

Quick Check

Count back to subtract.

1. $10 - 1 =$ _____   2. $8 - 2 =$ _____   3. $9 - 3 =$ _____

Write the difference.

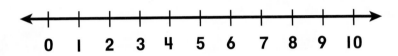

4. $\begin{array}{r} 8 \\ -3 \\ \hline \end{array}$ 5. $\begin{array}{r} 6 \\ -2 \\ \hline \end{array}$ 6. $\begin{array}{r} 7 \\ -1 \\ \hline \end{array}$ 7. $\begin{array}{r} 10 \\ -3 \\ \hline \end{array}$ 8. $\begin{array}{r} 5 \\ -1 \\ \hline \end{array}$ 9. $\begin{array}{r} 9 \\ -2 \\ \hline \end{array}$

Match.
Then subtract.

10. How many more  than ◯ ?

$8 - 6 =$ _____

Math Challenge

Duck Feet

Leon counts 10 feet.
How many ducks are there?

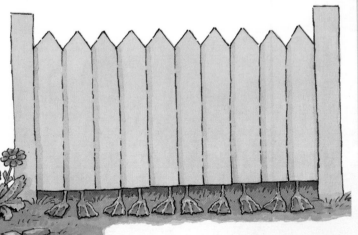

_____ ducks

Relate Addition and Subtraction

 MathTracks 1 / 18
Listen and Understand

Objective
Write and solve related addition and subtraction facts.

Vocabulary
related facts

These facts are **related facts.**
They have the same parts and wholes.

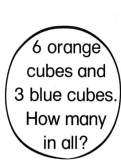

6 orange cubes and 3 blue cubes. How many in all?

Workmat 3
Whole

Part	Part

9 cubes. 3 are blue. How many orange?

Workmat 3
Whole
9

Part	Part

__6__ + __3__ = __9__   __9__ − __3__ = __6__

Guided Practice

Use 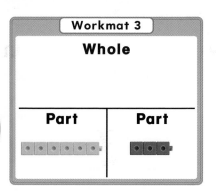 , and Workmat 3.
Show the parts. Complete the related facts.

Think
8 and 1 are the parts. I need to find the whole.

1. **8** and **1** ____ + ____ = ____   ____ − ____ = ____

2. **5** and **4** ____ + ____ = ____   ____ − ____ = ____

3. **4** and **6** ____ + ____ = ____   ____ − ____ = ____

TEST TIPS **Explain Your Thinking** How are the number sentences $5 + 2 = 7$ and $7 − 2 = 5$ related?

Remember that related facts have the same parts and wholes.

Use ▣ , ◼ , and Workmat 3.
Show the parts.
Complete the related facts.

1.

Whole	
Part	**Part**
▣▣▣▣	◼◼◼◼◼◼

$4 + 6 = \underline{10}$

$10 - 6 = \underline{4}$

2.

Whole	
Part	**Part**
▣▣▣	◼◼◼◼◼

$3 + 5 = \underline{}$

$8 - 5 = \underline{}$

3. 7 and 3 $\underline{} + \underline{} = \underline{}$ $\underline{} - \underline{} = \underline{}$

4. 2 and 7 $\underline{} + \underline{} = \underline{}$ $\underline{} - \underline{} = \underline{}$

5. $\begin{array}{r} 2 \\ +8 \\ \hline \end{array}$ $\begin{array}{r} 10 \\ -8 \\ \hline \end{array}$

6. $\begin{array}{r} 4 \\ +3 \\ \hline \end{array}$ $\begin{array}{r} 7 \\ -3 \\ \hline \end{array}$

7. $\begin{array}{r} 1 \\ +9 \\ \hline \end{array}$ $\begin{array}{r} 10 \\ -9 \\ \hline \end{array}$

Algebra Readiness ▶ Number Sentences

Write the difference.
Circle the related addition fact.

8. $\begin{array}{r} 10 \\ -4 \\ \hline \end{array}$

$6 + 4 = 10$
$5 + 4 = 9$

9. $\begin{array}{r} 9 \\ -5 \\ \hline \end{array}$

$5 + 5 = 10$
$4 + 5 = 9$

At Home Ask your child how the two facts in Exercise 7 are related.

Name_____

Fact Families

MathTracks 1/19
Listen and Understand

Objective
Write fact families using related facts.

Vocabulary
fact family

Related facts make a **fact family.**

This fact family uses the numbers 9, 5, and 4.

Whole	
9	
Part	**Part**
4	5

9 is the whole.
4 and 5 are the parts.

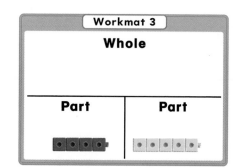

Workmat 3
Whole

Part	**Part**

___4___ + ___5___ = ___9___

___5___ + ___4___ = ___9___

Workmat 3
Whole

Part	**Part**

___9___ – ___5___ = ___4___

___9___ – ___4___ = ___5___

Guided Practice

Use  ,  , and Workmat 3.
Complete the fact family.

Think
I use 10, 6, and 4 to write the related facts.

1.

Whole	
10	
Part	**Part**
6	4

_____ + _____ = _____   _____ – _____ = _____

_____ + _____ = _____   _____ – _____ = _____

2.

Whole	
9	
Part	**Part**
6	3

_____ + _____ = _____   _____ – _____ = _____

_____ + _____ = _____   _____ – _____ = _____

TEST TIPS **Explain Your Thinking** What other fact is related to 4 + 4 = 8?

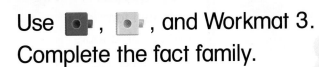

Use , , and Workmat 3.
Complete the fact family.

Remember that the two parts equal the whole.

1.

Whole
10

Part	Part
7	3

___7__ + ___3__ = __10__   __10__ − __3__ = __7__

_____ + _____ = _____   _____ − _____ = _____

2.

Whole
8

Part	Part
2	6

_____ + _____ = _____   _____ − _____ = _____

_____ + _____ = _____   _____ − _____ = _____

3.

Whole
10

Part	Part
2	8

_____ + _____ = _____   _____ − _____ = _____

_____ + _____ = _____   _____ − _____ = _____

4.

Whole
9

Part	Part
5	4

_____ + _____ = _____   _____ − _____ = _____

_____ + _____ = _____   _____ − _____ = _____

Algebra Readiness ▶ Missing Addends

Choose a number to complete
the number sentence.

| 5 | 6 | 7 |

5. ☐ + 4 = 10   6. ☐ + 3 = 10

At Home Ask your child to write a fact family
using the numbers 3, 4, and 7.

Name_____

Using Subtraction Strategies

MathTracks 1/20
Listen and Understand

Ways to Subtract

Count back
Use a number line
Draw a picture
Use a related addition fact

There are many ways to find a difference.

Guided Practice

Choose a way to subtract.
Write the difference.

1. $\begin{array}{r} 10 \\ -\ 3 \\ \hline \end{array}$

Think
I can count back 3. Say 10. Count 9, 8, 7.

2. $\begin{array}{r} 8 \\ -6 \\ \hline \end{array}$

3. $\begin{array}{r} 7 \\ -7 \\ \hline \end{array}$

4. $\begin{array}{r} 10 \\ -\ 2 \\ \hline \end{array}$

5. $\begin{array}{r} 10 \\ -\ 6 \\ \hline \end{array}$

6. $\begin{array}{r} 7 \\ -6 \\ \hline \end{array}$

7. $\begin{array}{r} 6 \\ -3 \\ \hline \end{array}$

8. $\begin{array}{r} 8 \\ -0 \\ \hline \end{array}$

9. $\begin{array}{r} 8 \\ -7 \\ \hline \end{array}$

10. $\begin{array}{r} 9 \\ -4 \\ \hline \end{array}$

11. $\begin{array}{r} 8 \\ -4 \\ \hline \end{array}$

12. $7 - 2 =$ _____

13. $10 - 4 =$ _____

14. $9 - 9 =$ _____

15. $10 - 5 =$ _____

16. $10 - 1 =$ _____

17. $9 - 5 =$ _____

TEST TIPS **Explain Your Thinking** How did you find $9 - 5$?

Choose a way to subtract.

Ways to Subtract

Count back
Use a number line
Draw a picture
Use a related addition fact

Write the difference.

1. 3
   −3
   ____
    0

2. 5
   −0
   ____

3. 2
   −1
   ____

4. 8
   −5
   ____

5. 7
   −5
   ____

6. 6
   −6
   ____

7. 9
   −7
   ____

8. 7
   −3
   ____

9. 9
   −0
   ____

10. 5
   −4
   ____

11. 10
   −10
   ____

12. 9
   −8
   ____

13. 9
   −3
   ____

14. 4
   −0
   ____

15. 6
   −4
   ____

16. 1
   −0
   ____

17. 9
   −6
   ____

18. 7
   −4
   ____

19. 7 − 0 = ____

20. 5 − 1 = ____

21. 10 − 8 = ____

22. 3 − 2 = ____

23. 6 − 5 = ____

24. 6 − 2 = ____

Problem Solving ▷ Logical Thinking

Use clues to find the number.

25. I am inside a shape.
    I am greater than 5.
    I am less than 9.
    I am not in the triangle.

    Which number am I? _____

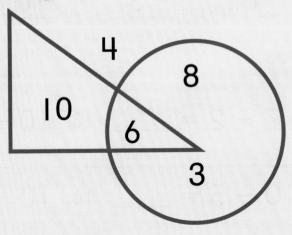

At Home Ask your child to explain how to subtract 10 − 4 using different strategies.

Choose the Operation

MathTracks 1/21
Listen and Understand

Objective
Solve problems by choosing the correct operation.

Use subtraction to solve a problem.

Think
I know the whole and one of the parts. I can subtract to find the other part.

9 sheep are eating grass.

1 sheep goes away.

How many sheep are there now?

sheep eating grass	
9	
sheep that go away	**sheep that are left**
1	

9	sheep
− 1	goes away
8	sheep now

Use addition to solve a problem.

Think
I know the parts. I can add to find the whole.

8 ducks are eating seeds.

2 more come to eat.

How many ducks are there in all?

number of ducks in all	
ducks eating seeds	**ducks that come**
8	2

	ducks
+	more
	ducks in all

Choose the operation to solve.

Draw or write to explain.

1. There are **8** horses in the barn. **2** horses leave. How many horses are in the barn now?

   Think
   I need to find how many are left.

   _____ horses

2. **5** cows are eating grass. **4** more join them to eat. How many cows are eating?

   Think
   I need to find how many in all.

   _____ cows

Practice

3. **9** pigs are in the pen. **3** pigs go away. How many pigs are left?

   _____ pigs

4. **4** chicks are eating. **4** more come to eat. How many chicks are eating in all?

   _____ chicks

Go on

Choose a Strategy

Solve.

1. There are **2** brown cows.
   There are **5** black cows.
   How many cows are there
   in all?

Draw or write to explain.

cow

_____ cows

2. **9** donkeys are outside.
   2 go into the barn.
   How many donkeys are
   outside now?

donkey

_____ donkeys

3. The farmer has **1** rooster.
   She gets **5** more roosters.
   How many roosters are
   there?

rooster

_____ roosters

4. **Multistep 8** goats are
   eating. **5** goats leave.
   Then, **2** goats come back
   to eat more. How many
   goats are eating now?

goat

_____ goats

At Home Create problems that your child
can solve by either adding or subtracting.

Listen to your teacher read the problem.
Solve.

1. There are **4** horses in one stable. There are **6** horses in another stable. How many horses are there in both stables?	Show your work using pictures, numbers, or words. _____ horses
2. There are **6** horses in the barn. **2** are taken out for a run. How many horses are still in the barn?	 _____ horses

Listen to your teacher read the problem.
Choose the correct answer.

3. 2   6   8   14
   ○   ○   ○   ○

4. 5   6   9   10
   ○   ○   ○   ○

Name _____

Find the sum and the difference.

1. 2 + 7 = ____

   9 − 7 = ____

2. 5 + 3 = ____

   8 − 3 = ____

Write the fact family.

3.
Whole
9

Part	Part
4	5

____ + ____ = ____   ____ − ____ = ____

____ + ____ = ____   ____ − ____ = ____

Write the difference.

4. 6
   −0
   ___

5. 7
   −2
   ___

6. 1 0
   − 5
   ___

7. 5
   −1
   ___

8. 4
   −4
   ___

Choose the operation to solve.

9. Rosita has 6 animal cards. Mark gives her 2 more animal cards. How many animal cards does Rosita have now?

Draw or write to explain.

_____ cards

Key Topic Review

Write the sum.

1. 8 + 1 = _____   2. 9 + 1 = _____   3. 7 + 3 = _____

4. 6 + 3 = _____   5. 8 + 2 = _____   6. 5 + 3 = _____

7. 4 + 5 = _____   8. 2 + 7 = _____   9. 3 + 4 = _____

10.   1
  +5

11.   5
  +4

12.   3
  +3

13.   2
  +8

14.   0
  +8

15.   1
  +7

Science Connection

Red Pandas

Red pandas live in the mountains in Asia.

In the morning, a red panda eats 10 bamboo leaves. In the afternoon, he eats 6 bamboo leaves.

How many more leaves does the panda eat in the morning than in the afternoon?

_____ leaves

WEEKLY WR **READER** eduplace.com/kids/mw/

Vocabulary *e • Glossary*

1. Which can you use to subtract $10 - 1$?
   Circle.

   | count on | count back |

2. What is this called?
   Circle.

   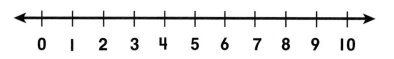

   | number line | fact family |

3. Write a **related fact** for $8 + 1 = 9$.

   ____ − ____ = ____

Concepts and Skills

Count back to subtract.

4. $10 - 1 =$ ____   5. $10 - 3 =$ ____   6. $8 - 2 =$ ____

Find the difference.

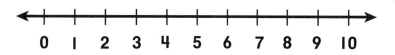

7. $9 - 2 =$ ____   8. $6 - 3 =$ ____   9. $7 - 1 =$ ____

Match. Then subtract.

10. How many more  than 🐷 are there?

$5 - 2 =$ ____

Complete the related facts.

11. 7   9
    +2   −2

12. 6   10
    +4   − 4

13. 5   9
    +4   −4

Complete the fact family.

14.

Whole
10

Part	Part
3	7

____ + ____ = ____   ____ − ____ = ____

____ + ____ = ____   ____ − ____ = ____

Write the difference.

15. 7
    −2

16. 10
    − 1

17. 5
    −1

18. 8
    −4

Problem Solving

Choose the operation to solve.

Draw or write to explain.

19. Kate sees 10 baby chicks. 6 chicks run away. How many chicks are left?

_____ chicks

20. On Monday Luca milks 3 cows. On Tuesday he milks 4 cows. How many cows does he milk in all?

_____ cows

166 one hundred sixty-six

National Zoo

WEEKLY WR READER®
Science Connection

Our country has a zoo called the National Zoo. Each animal has a home like the one it lived in before it came to the zoo.

This chart gives information about animals that live at the National Zoo.

Lowland Gorilla, National Zoo

Type of Animal	Number of Animals	Name of Zoo Home
Lowland gorilla	9	The Great Ape House
Ring-tailed lemur	8	Lemur Island
Giant panda	2	Asia Trail

Use the table to solve.

Draw or write to explain.

1. How many more animals live in The Great Ape House than on Lemur Island?

_____ more animal

2. How many lemurs and pandas live at the zoo in all?

_____ lemurs and pandas

3. How many more lemurs than pandas live at the zoo?

_____ more lemurs

Animals eat different foods.

- Lowland gorillas eat leaves, tree bark, and fruit.

- Ring-tailed lemurs eat bugs, leaves, and fruit.

- Giant pandas eat bamboo, fruit, and biscuits.

Write a number sentence to solve.

1. Teva sees **3** lemurs eating in one tree. She sees **5** lemurs eating in another tree. How many lemurs does she see altogether?

_____ + _____ = _____

_____ lemurs

2. There are **9** gorillas eating in The Great Ape House. **3** gorillas walk away. How many gorillas are still eating?

_____ − _____ = _____

_____ gorillas

3. Jamal sees **2** giant pandas and **4** ring-tailed lemurs. How many animals does he see in all?

_____ + _____ = _____

_____ animals

4. There are **9** gorillas at a zoo. **2** gorillas go to a zoo in another state. How many gorillas are left?

_____ − _____ = _____

_____ gorillas

 Technology

Visit *Education Place* at **eduplace.com/kids/mw/** to learn more about this topic.

168 one hundred sixty-eight

Unit 2 Test

Vocabulary *e • Glossary*

Complete the sentence.

double
number line
related fact

1. A _____ helps me add and subtract.

2. $2 + 2$ is a _____ fact.

3. _____ have the same parts and whole.

Concepts and Skills

Use an addition strategy.
Write the sum.

4. 8
   +2

5. 2
   +2

6. 9
   +1

7. 5
   +4

8. 1
   +6

9. 7
   +2

10. 6
    +0

11. 3
    +3

12. 8
    +1

13. 2
    +6

Use a subtraction strategy.
Write the difference.

14. 10
   − 0

15. 7
    −5

16. 8
    −8

17. 4
    −3

18. 9
    −4

19. 5
    −1

20. 9
    −6

21. 7
    −4

22. 6
    −3

23. 7
    −6

Unit 2 Test

Use ![cube], ![cube], and Workmat 3.
Show the parts. Complete the related facts.

24. 6 and 1   ____ + ____ = ____   ____ − ____ = ____

25. 2 and 7   ____ + ____ = ____   ____ − ____ = ____

26. 8 and 2   ____ + ____ = ____   ____ − ____ = ____

27. 5 + 3 = ____   28. 1 + 9 = ____

    8 − 3 = ____   10 − 1 = ____

Use ![cube], ![cube], and Workmat 3.
Complete the fact family.

29.

Whole
9

Part	Part
6	3

____ + ____ = ____   ____ − ____ = ____

____ + ____ = ____   ____ − ____ = ____

Problem Solving

Choose the operation to solve.

Draw or write to explain.

30. Rae sees 5 chickens eating.
3 more chickens come to
eat. How many chickens
are eating now?

____ chickens

170 one hundred seventy

Find the sum.

1. 4 + 2

Show your work using pictures, numbers, or words.

4 + 2 = ____

Find the difference.

2. 7 – 3

Show your work using pictures, numbers, or words.

7 – 3 = ____

Solve.

3. There are **5** frogs on a log. Then **2** more frogs come. How many frogs are there in all?

Show your work using pictures, numbers, or words.

_____ frogs

Estimating Sums and Differences

Circle the best estimate.

more than 7

1. 7 + 1

less than 7

2. 9 − 3

more than 9

less than 9

more than 5

3. 4 + 2

less than 5

4. 7 − 2

more than 6

less than 6

Estimate.

5. **Talk About It** Is 5 + 3 more than 6?
   Tell how you know.

6. About how many bugs are there?

   about _____

   Now count the bugs.
   How many bugs are there?   _____

   Write About It Was your estimate
   reasonable? Why?

   _____

   _____

Technology
Visit *Education Place* at
eduplace.com/kids/mw/ for
brain teasers.

Computer
Cubes to Add

Use the connecting cubes found at
eduplace.com/kids/mw/ to add.

Sam has 3 stamps. He finds 4 more. How many
stamps does Sam have in all?

1. Put your pointer over
   the **Stamp** tool.
   · Click the red cube 3 times.

2. Put your pointer over
   the **Stamp** tool.
   · Click the blue cube 4 times.

3. Click **[1 2 3]**.

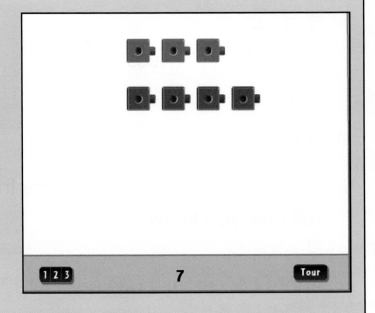

Use the cubes.
Write each sum.

1. 2 + 3 = _____

2. 4 + 5 = _____

3. There are 2 girls and 4 boys
   in line. How many children
   are in line?

   _____ children

4. Tim draws 3 circles and 1
   square. How many shapes
   does Tim draw?

   _____ shapes

Test-Taking Tips
• •

Work slowly.

Check your work.

If you are not sure how to find the answer, go on to the next question.

Multiple Choice

Fill in the ○ for the correct answer.

1. Count on to add.

$$7$$
$$+2$$

3	5	7	9
○	○	○	○

2. Use a double fact to add.

$$4$$
$$+5$$

6	7	8	9
○	○	○	○

3. What number is 2 more than 4?

←——+——+——+——+——+——+——+——+——+——+——→
0   1   2   3   4   5   6   7   8   9   10

4	6	7	8
○	○	○	○

4. Look at the pictograph. How many children choose bears?

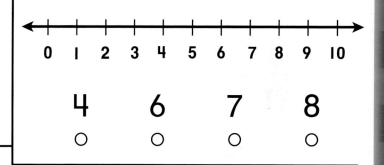

Favorite Animals

3	4	5	6
○	○	○	○

Fill in the ○ for the correct answer.
N means not here.

5. Count back to subtract.

$$10 - 3$$

7	6	5	N
○	○	○	○

6. How many more
than  ?

1	2	3	4
○	○	○	○

7. Which number is greater
than 7?

9	7	5	3
○	○	○	○

Solve.

8. There are 2 ducks in the
water. 3 more ducks come.
How many ducks are there
in all?

_____ ducks

Write the number sentence.

_____

9. Write this fact another way.

$$6 + 2 = 8$$

_____

10. How many children
choose fish?

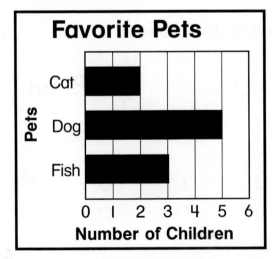

_____ children

Test Prep on the Net
Visit *Education Place* at
eduplace.com/kids/mw/
for more test prep practice.